in-laws, outlaws, *and* granny flats

in-laws, outlaws, *and* granny flats

YOUR GUIDE TO TURNING
ONE HOUSE INTO TWO HOMES

Michael Litchfield

The Taunton Press

The Taunton Press
Inspiration for hands-on living®

The Taunton Press, Inc.,
63 South Main Street,
PO Box 5506, Newtown, CT 06470-5506
e-mail: tp@taunton.com

Editors: Mark Feirer, Peter Chapman
Copy editor: Anne Jones
Indexer: Jay Kreider
Cover and Interior design: Teresa Fernandes
Layout: Laura Lind Design
Illustrator: Martha Garstang Hill
Photographer: Muffy Kibbey, except where noted on p. 216
Front cover photographer: Eric Roth

The following names/manufacturers appearing in *In-laws, Outlaws, and Granny Flats* are trademarks: Basement Systems®, Chevy®, CoolDrawer®, DELTA®-DRAIN, Delta Touch 20®, ENERGY STAR®, GacoFlex®, GE Advantium®, GROHE® Freehander®, Häfele®, Hansgrohe®, IKEA®, InSoFast®, LiftBed®, Marmoleum®, Murphy Bed Company™, Owens Corning®, Oxygenic®, Porcher®, Porsche®, Rev-a-Shelf®, Safety Tubs®, Sorotube®, Thermax™, TOTO® Aqua®, TOTO® Washlet®, YesterTec®.

Library of Congress Cataloging-in-Publication Data
Litchfield, Michael W.
  In-laws, outlaws, and granny flats : your guide to turning one house into two homes / Michael W. Litchfield.
    p. cm.
  Includes index.
  ISBN 978-1-60085-251-0
  1. Dwellings--Remodeling. 2. Buildings--Additions. I. Title.
  TH4816.2.L58 2011
  643'.7--dc22

                    2010050267

Printed in the United States of America
10 9 8 7 6 5 4 3 2

Homebuilding is inherently dangerous. From accidents with power tools to falls from ladders, scaffolds, and roofs, builders risk serious injury and even death. We try to promote safe work habits throughout this book, but what is safe for one person under certain circumstances may not be safe for you under different circumstances. So don't try anything you learn about here (or elsewhere) unless you're certain that it is safe for you. If something about an operation doesn't feel right, don't do it. Look for another way. Please keep safety foremost in your mind whenever you're working.

acknowledgments

A NUMBER OF KIND AND EXCEPTIONALLY TALENTED PEOPLE made this book possible, starting with architect Fran Halperin, whose clever drawings and deep knowledge guided my efforts from beginning to end. Thanks also to Stephen Shoup of buildingLab, Robin Pennell and his colleagues at Jarvis Architects, Russ Hamlet, Eric Christ, Dean & Marty Rutherford, Chip Harley, Riley Doty, Steve Rynerson, Alan Jenks, Lynn Hopkins, Mike Davis, Tim and Lisa Goodman, and Michael McAlister. Special thanks to Carol Berg, Housing Manager for the City of Santa Cruz, for graciously sharing her insights and contacts.

Thanks to the scores of homeowners who shared their stories and invited me in; many are listed below. Getting to know you was the best part of creating this book. Fond thanks to the Foster family for showing what neighbors can accomplish together.

George and Sally Kiskaddon of Builders Booksource gave me sound advice early and late. It was a pleasure to work with Muffy Kibbey, whose beautiful photos grace this book. Photographer Art Grice also gave it his best. And kudos to illustrator Martha Garstang Hill.

Thanks to all my Taunton Press colleagues who work so hard, among them Maria Taylor, Allison Hollett, Katy Binder, Chuck Miller, and John Ross. Mark Feirer's tenacity made this a much better book. And especially Senior Editor Peter Chapman, without whose vision this book would have never happened at all: Thanks for everything, Peter.

Lastly, love and gratitude to my sweetheart, Jeannie. And the dog, Louie, who kept me from staying too long at the desk. May there always be a dog.

—Michael Litchfield
Point Reyes, California

AND THANKS TO...

Drew Allen, Kobe Allen, Leticia Allen, Monica Allen, Keith Alward, Brajit Bacon, Cooke Bedford, Aya Brackett, Heidi and Jim Bye, Kelly Cash, Theresa Cassagne, Ovidio Cruz, Paul DeGroot, Kathryn DeLaszlo, Gene Desmidt, David Edrington, Bard Foster, David Foster and Margot McBane, Eleanor and Herbert Foster, Etta Foster, Ken Foster, Onawa Foster, Amy Gardner, Donna and George Gerhold, Charlotte and Michael Green, Tina Govan, Scott Grice, Susan and Art Hartinger, Julie Heine, Jeff Hellerman, Keith Hernandez, Amy Hutton, Michael Janzen, Bill Jetton, Deb Kadas, Lloyd Kahn, Nancy Kimura and Marc Birnbaum, Jim Kravets, Clay Lucchesi, Gino Lucchesi, Lisa Lum and Michael Hohmeyer, Richard Maestas, Stephen Marshall, Elizabeth Martin, Anagabriela Hernandez McKig, Billie McKig, Suzie McKig, Michael Mery, Cherie Mohr, Anne Murphy, Lawrence and Monica Ponoroff, Sue Rodgerson, Chipper Roth, Devin Rutkowski, Mary Ann and Edward Scheuer, Taya Shoup, Tim Snyder, Nancy Stein, Beth and Gary Sumner, Rob Thallon, Renee Torres, Ann and Larry Tramutola, Sarah and Darrell Valor, Sim van der Ryn, Roxana Vargas-Greenan, Jean-Paul Vellotti, Serge Vigeant, Bill Welte, and Jane White.

contents

introduction

I N THE THIRTY-SOME YEARS I'VE BEEN RENOVATING HOUSES or writing about them, I've owned six—in rural Vermont, suburban Connecticut, and northern California—fixing each one up and then moving on. Now I live on a sweet piece of land that was once a small dairy farm above Tomales Bay, which empties into the Pacific. The farmer built his house on this gentle hillside because his cows found it peaceful here. So do I.

It's a different living arrangement than any I've tried before because the property has two homes on it: a main house (the original farmhouse) and an in-law unit. The in-law evolved from a pair of outbuildings that once housed tractors and other agricultural paraphernalia. I live in the in-law part, which has 12-ft. ceilings and quarry tile floors throughout, and though it's a bit smaller than my other homes, it's comfortable, affordable, and more than big enough for my life.

And it's nice having a neighbor close by. We don't see each other very often—no more often than you'd see a neighbor across a fence—but every now and then we stop and chat or maybe share a chore.

A TRADITION RETURNS

The longer I live in this shared arrangement, the more I like it, which made me wonder why more people don't live this way. Well, as it turns out, they do. Although there hasn't been much written about secondary dwelling units, they have a long pedigree and are remarkably widespread. You'll find shared housing setups through-out the world, especially where extended families share a roof. Even in North America, several generations under one roof was a widespread living arrangement until a post–World War II building boom made single-family houses with white picket fences the American Dream.

But times change. As houses got larger, family sizes shrank and energy got more expensive. And as Baby Boomers age, our ideas of the good life and the ideal house have changed, too. For example, homeowners who have added in-law units feel that they now have more lifestyle choices, greater economic security, and deeper personal satisfaction, according to several academic studies and a ground-breaking 2000 AARP white paper (see Resources on p. 214). So if their experiences are any guide, in-law housing is a great idea whose time has come again.

ONE HOUSE, TWO HOMES, MANY SOLUTIONS

One of the most striking things about in-laws is how varied and flexible they are. This book contains the stories of many families with in-law units, yet as different as each one is, even these solutions barely scratch the surface of what's possible. Having an in-law suite can help you:

- **Become more economically secure.** Whether you want to save money for retirement or use rental income to defray mortgage payments and property taxes, an in-law unit can help you do it. An in-law apartment is a tangible asset you can keep an eye on.
- **Allow an elderly or infirm parent to live independently on your property,** thus enhancing their quality of life—and yours. Giving children a chance to get to know their grandparents is one of the most frequently cited benefits of in-law housing.

- **Trade lodging for services.** By reducing or trading the rent of your in-law suite, you can get a tenant who's willing to look after your children, maintain your property, help with housework, or provide care for an aged parent.

- **Provide a safe landing place** for an adult child who's changing careers, going through a life change, or who can't yet afford a place of his or her own. The right in-law configuration will create enough space, support, and privacy for everyone.

- **Afford a house.** For some first-time homeowners, the projected income from an in-law unit will enable them to buy a house they couldn't afford otherwise.

- **Shorten your commute.** Many in-law suites double as home offices, allowing owners to spend more time with their families and less time stuck in traffic. This is particularly appealing to those who want to live in an environmentally responsible manner.

- **Bring the world home.** Inviting relatives and out-of-town friends for an extended stay is another popular use of in-law suites, particularly if you can't travel because you have new babies, a busy schedule, or mobility issues. Companionship is a boon for all ages.

- **See the world.** Several homeowners profiled in this book plan to rent out their main house and travel once their kids leave home. Those adventurers will have money to travel with, a tenant to keep an eye on the house, and a place to stash their stuff.

- **Rekindle a romance.** One still-young couple with four children bought their new house precisely because it had a large in-law suite downstairs, in the back of the house—far from the four upstairs bedrooms where the kids would sleep.

- **Express yourself.** Because in-law units are modestly sized, they're often more

fun to design. One retired homeowner relished the task because, she noted, "It's the first space I've ever had all to myself, so I'm going to make it extra nice."

- **Stick around while renovating the big house.** Living in a house that's being renovated is like living in a war zone, and renting another place is expensive. If you can retreat to your in-law, however, you're home free.

- **Build and live green.** Thanks to their compact size, in-laws are, inherently,

among the greenest ways to live, especially when built with green materials and energy-conserving appliances.

Well, that's a start. In this book, we'll visit with some folks who have created in-law units—to learn what life issues prompted their interest, what practical considerations guided their choices, and how things turned out for them. Creating an in-law is eminently about making smart decisions and finding clever solutions, but it's also about compassion, community, and a love of beauty—as you'll see in every one of the in-laws in this book. Who knows? You may be inspired to create an in-law unit of your own. Should that be the case, the first four chapters—which go from assessing your needs to applying for permits—should get you off to a good start.

Bump-out additions are often a cost-effective way to create an in-law unit, and because construction is isolated to the addition, they're less disruptive than a basement or attic conversion.

is an in-law unit right for you?

ONE OF THE KEY REQUIREMENTS of any successful home design is that it fit the people who live in it. Thus, any designers or architects worth their salt will start with many questions about how their clients live: what they do for work and how they relax, how much time they spend with friends and family, how they see their lives 10 or 20 years down the road, and so on. Designing an in-law unit is largely the same process, except that it often requires a greater degree of empathy—for the people who will live in it and for the neighbors who will be living next to it.

Chapter 2 gets into the nitty-gritty of selecting an in-law design but, here, let's spend a little time thinking about the social arrangement you create when you build an in-law unit. In fact, let's start by looking at some of your traits and assumptions. Ultimately, adding a successful in-law will depend on how good a fit it is for you.

TWO HOMES, COMMON GROUND

There are many good reasons to add an in-law, but to get the benefits you'll have to trade some of your privacy and space. Whether that new person on your property is a close relative or a rental tenant, he or she will impact your life in some way.

Adding an in-law unit and sharing your property will require a period of adjustment, especially if you've lived in the house for a long time. However, good design and careful planning can go a long way toward creating

SHARING YOUR SPACE: 11 QUESTIONS TO CONSIDER

This list explores how sociable you are, how much control you need, and how much experience you've had living with others.

1. How many siblings did you grow up with?
2. How much of last week's downtime was spent with friends?
3. Do you schedule regular get-togethers with friends? (These might include seeing a movie, going to church groups, or having beers after a workout at the gym.)
4. How relaxed are you about your material possessions? Do friends have any of your books, tools, cooking equipment, food containers?
5. When you go to a restaurant, do you share what you order?
6. If someone cuts in front of you in traffic or in a theater line, how do you react?
7. When was the last time you had a fight with a neighbor? What was it about?
8. Is your work mostly solitary or social? Tightly focused or multitasked?
9. Where are you on the "Speak My Mind vs. Keep It to Myself" continuum?
10. Have you ever shared a house with someone who wasn't family or a loved one?
11. Do you live with someone or alone? How long have you lived that way?

In general, people who have siblings, aren't super-fussy, can multitask, and don't sweat the small stuff have an easier time sharing their property. Communicating freely is the key to defusing conflicts.

two compatible, comfortable dwellings that coexist peacefully. Thoughtful construction details indoors and out can make a new unit seem like it has always been right there; new landscaping helps to complete the effect.

The success of an in-law also depends on whom you share it with, and how. If the person is a relative, you'll probably know a lot about their personality. Renting to a tenant is pretty much the opposite situation, but working through your personal networks is the best way

Many young adults and families just starting out find that in-law units provide a cost-effective and convenient place to live. In nice weather, the 8-ft.-wide sliding door of this unit opens the kitchen to the deck.

to find someone you'll be comfortable having around. Likewise, there's a world of difference between sharing your property with a freestanding in-law cottage and sharing space in your house.

Keeping a tenant is much like keeping a friend. Be personable and stay engaged. If someone does something that bugs you, be kind but clear the air. Don't let things fester. And always have those difficult conversations face-to-face. At the same time, any healthy relationship requires a balance of intimacy and detachment. Have a life of your own and don't become overly dependent on each other. In like manner, respect your tenant's privacy and keep your distance. And whenever possible, make them feel at home—it may be *your* in-law but it's *their* home.

SHARED HOUSING: BACK TO THE FUTURE

For thousands of years, extended families have lived together, whether sharing a home or family compound, and in large parts of the world that's still the way things are. (Shared housing is common in Europe; in Asia and Latin America, three-quarters of the elderly live with children.) In 1860, roughly 80 percent of Americans 65 or older lived in a house with their children or in the house next door. Typically, parents aged in place and, in time, the next generation would inherit the property. Back then most people worked the land. Farms and ranches required a lot of labor, so hired hands were also part of those extended families, though they were usually housed separately. The oldest in-law unit in this book, the Murphy Ranch bunkhouse (see p. 14), built in 1857, was typical.

As Western Europe and North America became industrialized, however, farmers became factory hands, families got smaller, and the percentage of multigenerational households steadily declined for decades—with one exception: during the Great Depression. To weather that storm, families pooled resources and shared houses, and some homeowners took boarders. But for the additional income from renters, many more families would have defaulted on their mortgages and lost their homes.

After World War II, the percentage of multigenerational housing resumed its decline. The nuclear family housing boom was on, thanks to government-subsidized loans to veterans, cheap land, an improving economy, and a young generation eager to start families. That flight to the suburbs often meant leaving elderly parents behind, but because of Social Security, which began in 1936, elderly people could often afford to live on their own. The statistics are spotty, but by 1990, less than 15 percent of elderly Americans lived with their kids. But that's changing.

According to the 2000 census, the percentage of multigenerational households increased—for the first time in more than a century—and by 2008 that number was up 12 percent from its low point. The shift reflected not only elders moving in with their kids, but also young adults who perhaps had never left home: more than a third of Americans 18 to 34 now live with their parents. This shift was partly economic, partly cultural (Asian and Latin American newcomers have far stronger kinship bonds), and partly spiritual. For many people, the Age of McMansions was an empty time. So perhaps our new interest in shared housing is also a search for something more satisfying, soulful, and sustainable.

Designing small spaces often leads to creative uses of nontraditional materials. A pair of recycled steel shipping containers (below) provided the structure for one project. When complete (bottom), it featured cork flooring over a radiant heating system, with horizontal strips of recycled fir paneling on the walls.

SMART CITIES, INTELLIGENT IN-LAWS

In response to a number of housing-related crises, and as an antidote to urban sprawl, "smart-growth" advocates promote *urban infill*—adding housing units in areas already close to downtown shopping areas, community facilities, and mass transit. In-law units are an important element of any infill program because they add housing units to single-family lots in residential neighborhoods.

Communities benefit, too. Open land is preserved. When more people use municipal services, a city's per-resident costs go down, and city revenues are augmented by property taxes on new units. Because in-law units are typically small, their rents are often modest, too, increasing the pool of affordable housing for seniors, students, and service providers such as teachers, nurses, and elder-care workers. When located in older neighborhoods, in-law units are frequently within walking distance of downtown services. Moreover, because private owners create that affordable housing, cities needn't tap their limited resources to do so.

And because they are built on existing parcels and often built within an existing footprint, in-law units are among the greenest ways to build. They're smaller and so require fewer resources to build, operate, and maintain. They don't consume additional land—they use existing land more efficiently. And homeowners can create a second household for a fraction of the cost of a traditional house.

A GOLDEN EXAMPLE

Given this wealth of benefits, it's not surprising that smart-growth advocates, green builders, and just plain folks have pushed municipalities to revise zoning laws to make it easier for homeowners to build in-law units. One of the most remarkable successes is the city of Santa Cruz's Accessory Dwelling Unit (ADU) Development Program, in which this California city streamlined the permit and approval process, reduced fees, created manuals that walked homeowners through the development process, and created a set of seven prototype plan sets, which, if followed, resulted in an automatically approved in-law unit. As remarkable, this comprehensive program was developed in response to grass-roots community organizing (see p. 90).

In 2003, the same year Santa Cruz enacted its program, the California Assembly passed a bill (AB 1866) that required all cities and counties to allow ADUs "as a by-right option" for property owners, further encouraging the creation of such units.

IS THE WELCOME MAT OUT IN YOUR TOWN?

If an in-law unit seems like it might be a good match for you, find out what's allowed in your neighborhood. If in-law units already exist in your community, that's a good sign. A good place to start your search is the city's website, which often divides the city into districts or zones and describes what's allowed in each.

If you're web-shy, you can call the city planning department to get an informed (but informal) opinion from a planner. Typically, the planner will ask for your street address or parcel number and then direct you to (or mail you) the rules for your area. In most cases, the planner will end the conversation by noting that the planning commission or zoning official has the final say on your specific project.

After you check local zoning requirements for in-law units (see the chart on p. 12), you'll need to develop a design for your unit and find someone to build it. You might have the skills to do some or all of the work, or you might decide to hire professionals to do some or all of it. Chapter 4 spells out the roles and responsibilities of architects and contractors, while also explaining how to assemble a team to get the job done.

Personally, I recommend that you engage a local architect or designer-builder. Wading through all the building codes and zoning regulations can be overwhelming to someone who hasn't done it before. Moreover, local designers and architects will be familiar with products and building materials that are readily available in your area, and can give you a heads-up on costs.

FINDING THE MONEY

When it comes to financing an in-law unit, get information from as many sources as you can, starting with your financial adviser. Talk to your local bank and compare its offerings to those on the Internet. And talk to architects, contractors, and friends who have recently renovated their homes—in short, anyone with ground-level experience in financing a project. Here are some specifics to consider.

CONSIDER REFINANCING

If your home has substantial equity, refinancing your first mortgage might be the best bet. Home equity loans are less hassle than construction loans. Given the recent erosion of home prices, your lender may want a new appraisal on your house, but once the loan is approved you can spend the money as you like. A construction loan, on the other hand, requires that you submit a set of architectural drawings beforehand, costs more money to produce loan documents, and requires periodic site visits from bank officials before the bank will release funds. If you'll be working with a small contractor without large cash flows or if you're doing some of the work yourself, waiting for construction loan payouts can be a huge headache.

POOL RESOURCES

If you're building a unit for a parent, consider combining your resources with your parents' to fund the project. Plan ahead so that a sudden event such as an illness doesn't force you into selling assets at an inopportune time. Pooling resources can also help you afford a larger property or a home in a nicer neighborhood, if you or your parent is relocating to a new area.

ALWAYS TRY TO STAY WITHIN THE EXISTING FOOTPRINT when renovating a house or in-law unit. If you don't enlarge the square footage of the structure, you'll be more likely to save money and simplify code compliance—especially if the unit is nonconforming (see the bottom sidebar on the facing page).

COMMON ZONING STANDARDS FOR IN-LAW UNITS

Drawn from municipal codes around the country, this table summarizes the more common zoning standards governing in-law units. However, always follow the latest standards for your community.

CODE ISSUES	TYPICAL SPECS	IMPLICATIONS/COMMENTS
OWNER OCCUPANCY. Property owner must live in house or in-law unit.		Owner can't rent out both units, thus has a stake in finding responsible tenants, maintaining property.
MINIMUM LOT SIZE. Can't build in-law unit on lot smaller than minimum sq. ft. specified by city.	5,000 sq. ft.	Keeps neighborhood from becoming too dense. Lots above minimum size may be allowed to have larger (or detached) units.
MAXIMUM LOT COVERAGE. Combined areas for house and in-law unit can't exceed a certain percentage of the lot.	30% to 40%	Owner must balance space allocated to house and in-law unit in order to avoid overbuilding the lot.
MAXIMUM UNIT SIZE. (Minimum unit size may also be specified.) Deck usually not included in calculation.	750 sq. ft. maximum	Unit size may also be specified as a % of the house size. In effect, small units limit the number of tenants.
MAXIMUM HEIGHT OF UNIT. Height depends upon type of structure.	12 ft. for cottage, 22 ft. for over-garage unit	Too-tall units can dwarf houses next door, block sun, compromise privacy, destroy the scale of the neighborhood.
SETBACKS. Minimum distance from property lines along front, back, side yards. Same as house setbacks.	Front 20 ft.; back 10 ft.; side 5 ft.	Setbacks help to prevent spread of fire, ensure access, reduce privacy and noise impact on neighbors.
DETACHED/ATTACHED. Determines if unit may be attached to house.		Prohibiting *detached* units means less privacy between dwellings. Prohibiting *attached* units means you need a larger lot on which to build.
MINIMUM DISTANCE BETWEEN DWELLINGS. (Detached unit allowed.)	10 ft.	Distance between in-law unit and storage shed or garage may be less.
MAIN ENTRY/EGRESS. Location of unit's front door in relation to street, main house front door, or neighbor.	Both entries can't face the street unless unit door is screened from view.	Varies greatly from town to town. Locating entries of attic and basement conversions may be problematic.
INTERIOR AMENITIES. Kitchen or second bedroom may not be allowed.	A kitchen is the room most often disallowed.	Prevents an in-law unit from being a self-contained unit; limits rentability.
PARKING. Add parking space(s) for unit, can't reduce existing spaces.	Need at least 2 parking spaces for house, 1 additional for in-law unit.	May specify number of spaces to be added, whether they must be covered, whether cars may be parked in tandem in the drive. May determine if garage can be converted into an in-law unit.
CONDITIONAL PERMIT. Conditional use and building permits required.		More complicated review process. Meeting code requirements may not guarantee right to build in-law unit.
SAFETY-RELATED. Codes protect health and safety of occupants.	Follow local building codes.	Windows large and low enough to climb out of, smoke detectors and hard-wired alarms, exterior exit for all second units, structural reinforcement in quake zones, etc.
LESS COMMON STANDARDS		
GRANDFATHER PROVISION. Older, nonconforming units may be allowed, with certain restrictions.	Owner can't aggravate a nonconforming condition.	Usually a setback or lot-coverage issue. Renovation can't enlarge or move unit closer to property line.
SPECIAL STUDY ZONES. These include watershed, slide, earthquake fault zones.		The more restrictions a zone has, the more difficult it will be to modify or develop your property.
EXTERIOR FINISH. Details of in-law unit must match those of house.	Siding, trim, roof pitch should match that of house.	Finish details help the unit to blend in and give the neighborhood a consistent aesthetic style.
UTILITIES. May require separate utility connections for unit.	Rare	Tapping into existing service okay in most locales, which reduces costs.
STORAGE. Supplemental on-site storage for in-law unit.	Rare	Acknowledges that small in-law unit may not have adequate storage.

SHOP AROUND

Construction loans alone come in a dizzying number of forms including 30-year or 15-year fixed loans, adjustable-rates with 1- to 10-year terms, and rollover loans that can be refinanced into conventional mortgages once construction is done. There are also non-construction-specific products such as reverse-mortgages for seniors who have a lot of equity in their homes. Three things to note: The better your credit score and the greater your assets, the better terms you'll get. A construction loan can be complex, though, so seek out a loan officer experienced in such loans. Lastly, keep in mind that many loan officers are salespeople: always have your financial advisers review a lender's recommendations.

INVESTIGATE LOCAL PROGRAMS

There are many government programs to increase affordable housing, often administered by city or county agencies. Because in-law units can help cities meet affordable housing goals, homeowners creating in-laws may be eligible for development grants. In some areas, low-interest ADU loans are available from programs managed jointly by a city agency and, say, a local credit union. Canadian readers should look into the Canada Mortgage and Housing Corporation's extensive website (see Appendix, p. 212).

BUILD GREEN

Using energy-conserving materials and appliances is a smart way to reduce your unit's operating costs, and building green can generate rebates and tax credits. Tax credits for improving home energy efficiency have broad bipartisan support in Congress, so they're likely to be around for a while. The economic stimulus bill of 2009, for example, included 30% tax credits up to $1,500 total for products such as replacement windows, insulation, and sealants, and for energy-efficient furnaces, water heaters, air-conditioning, and so on. If you opt for a renewable energy source such as solar panels or geothermal heat pumps, you can get a 30% tax rebate on the installation—with no cap!—on any system installed till 2016.

COMPARING COSTS: RENOVATION VS. NEW CONSTRUCTION

Renovation is often more costly than new construction because damage and decay is often hidden under the wall surface, and you never know what you'll find until you open the walls. In addition to its unpredictability, renovation often involves "unbuilding" something—demolition—before you can complete the task you set out to do. Hence, higher labor costs frequently offset the "savings" of reusing existing materials. However, if studs are exposed and there are no surprises—if, say, you're converting an unfinished garage into an in-law—then renovation costs should actually be somewhat less than new construction.

IT'S PERFECTLY LEGAL to combine federal tax credits, state credits, and local utility rebates for energy-saving work done on your home or in-law unit. In fact, many agencies encourage homeowners to piggyback such incentives.

the in-law on the range

The story of the Murphy Ranch in-law features a colorful cast that includes cowboys and Indians; a family with six daughters and a tenant with 30 dogs; Italian, Irish, and Chinese ranch hands; and a modest redwood-framed structure that has watched them all come and go.

Shortly after California became a state and the title to land on northern California's Point Reyes Peninsula was wrested from the original Spanish grantees, a pair of Yankee lawyers, the Shafter brothers, ended up owning most

A classic bump-out addition, the Murphy Ranch bunkhouse (center, with chimney) sits above Home Creek. Built in 1857, it was rehabilitated in 2001.

Ranch workers with a little time on their hands don the gloves, spar a bit, and get ready for the 1936 Olympics.

Floor Plan

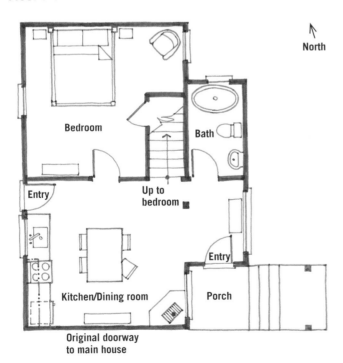

North

Bedroom

Bath

Entry

Up to bedroom

Kitchen/Dining room

Entry

Porch

Original doorway to main house

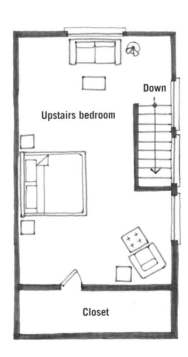

Down

Upstairs bedroom

Closet

In more than a century and a half, the Murphy Ranch in-law has housed ranch hands, family, and visitors. In that time, only two families have owned the ranch. Here, Anne Murphy confers with Gino and Clay.

of the peninsula. In 1857, they constructed a ranch house and various other buildings in a fertile valley fed by a year-round stream, Home Creek, where the Miwok Indians had lived for millennia.

Living in the bunkhouse—the in-law unit of its day—was a job perk conferred on ranch hands who had proven their worth. New arrivals and unproven hands slept in a barn or an outbuilding, and a surprising number of them were foreign-born: waves of Swiss Italians or Irish farmers fleeing famine or Chinese who'd come to work on the railroad. As farm lodgings went, the bunkhouse was pretty cushy. Partitioned into tiny rooms, it offered each man a modicum of privacy and a bed. And because one doorway opened into the dining annex of the main house, bunkhouse inhabitants generally got to the breakfast table first. It also had its own woodstove that cowboys could sit around and shoot the breeze if they weren't too exhausted from working dawn to dusk.

Like a modern in-law suite, the bunkhouse gave its dwellers a little distance from the family in the big house—and vice versa. This physical separation was especially welcome if, for example, the tenant farmer had six eligible daughters, as the DeFraga family did. No doubt, there was friction from time to time, but generally everyone got along. In fact, this social and economic arrangement was so stable that in 154 years, just two families have owned the ranch: the Shafters and then the Murphys.

THE MODERN WORLD CATCHES UP

But the bunkhouse's days as a cowboy dorm were numbered. Beef cattle required fewer hands than dairy cows, the ranch became more mechanized, and, thanks to automobiles, workers no longer had to live on the ranch. Sometime after World War II, the doorway into the main house was walled up, a few partitions were removed to open up the space, and a kitchen was installed downstairs (see photo below). By that time, the bunkhouse housed just one elderly hand, Jim Bernoud, his wife, and about 30 dogs. The Bernouds lived there till the 1970s, when they passed away and an era died with them.

Today, Home Creek still flows and a Murphy still runs the ranch. The property is now part of the Point Reyes National Seashore, and the bunkhouse lives on as an in-law apartment rented out to visitors who want to live on a working farm or explore surrounding parklands. In 2001, the National Park Service raised and repaired the building and gave it the foundation it never had, as well as a sweet little porch facing east. Now the bunkhouse sits high and dry above the creek and, with any luck, it will survive well into the next century. □

The exposed redwood joists and fir floors make the kitchen a warm place to hang out even when nothing's cooking. A doorway to the main house, hidden behind the red cabinet, was walled up when the building became a self-contained in-law unit.

When ranch hands lived here, the bunkhouse was divided into a labyrinth of tiny bedrooms upstairs and down. When the structure was renovated, the partitions were removed to open up the space and let in light.

The in-law has one large bedroom downstairs, and a larger one upstairs that runs the length of the building. Because drywall would be too slick for the rustic interior, the owners covered bedroom walls with salvaged redwood siding instead.

Redwood stairs were sculpted by a century and a half of ranch-hand feet.

KEEPING WATER AT BAY

What locals now know as the Murphy Ranch was well built for its day: its longevity attests to that. But the bunkhouse was poorly sited, constructed without a foundation, and inadequately maintained. Below, five tips to keep your home and in-law comfortable and dry.

- Keep your roof in good repair. Fix leaks immediately.

- Cut back vegetation away from the house. Plants retain moisture. And don't drench the siding when you water the area.

- Investigate any signs of water damage. Water stains around doors and windows may mean they aren't properly flashed.

- Slope the ground so water runs away from the house.

- Clean gutters and downspouts as needed. That's the single easiest way to reduce basement moisture problems.

After decades of deferred maintenance and exposure to periodic spring floods, the sills, first-floor joists, and many of the studs had rotted away.

CHAPTER 2

designing
in-laws

IN THIS CHAPTER, we'll consider the ingredients that go into a successfully designed in-law unit, one that works for homeowners, tenants, and neighbors. This last constituency—neighbors—often has the first say in the process, via the city planning department and the codes it oversees. Zoning codes are created, in part, to minimize potential conflicts between neighbors. Equally important are the unstated rules of conduct we observe in dealing with the folks next door or down the street, the little courtesies and concessions that keep the peace and affirm our

need to pull together. For that reason, our exploration into designing in-laws starts with a walk around the block.

FEELING AT HOME IN THE 'HOOD

If you've lived in your neighborhood for a while, you probably know it pretty well. But if you've just started to think about constructing an in-law unit, answering the questions below may help you see your community in a whole new light. Hopefully, your answers will help you decide which type of in-law unit fits in best and best fits your needs.

NEIGHBORHOOD QUESTIONS

- **Are neighborhood lots generously sized or small?** A 5,000-sq.-ft. urban lot is average; 7,500- to 10,000-sq.-ft. lots would be considered generous. In the suburbs, however, 10,000 sq. ft. might be considered small.
- **Are the spaces between houses generous or small?** In urban areas, 10 ft. between houses is generous.
- **Are the houses separated by fences or vegetation?**
- **Do neighboring lots have multiple buildings on them,** such as garden cottages, sheds, or detached garages?
- **Are houses more or less the same height** and size or do they vary widely?
- **How uniform are house styles?** Are roof pitches and exterior details (siding, windows, and so on) similar?
- **How are houses situated on their lots?** Do they cluster uniformly toward the front or back—this is called *massing*—or is their location more random?
- **How is parking handled?** Is it primarily in attached garages, detached garages, a driveway, or in spaces cut into the yard?
- **Are in-law units common in your neighborhood?** Is one type more common than others? Typically, how do

The size and shape of your lot will largely determine what type of in-law you can build. Here, a deep lot easily accommodates a detached unit.

tenants access their dwellings—are in-law entrances close to the street or must units be accessed via a path through the property?

SITE-SPECIFIC QUESTIONS

- **Is your parcel large or small, flat or sloped, wet or dry?** Is there standing water after heavy storms or during the rainy season? Is it in a special zone indicating that it's more susceptible to earthquake or slide activity?

■ **What shape is your lot:** long and narrow, squarish, irregular?

■ **If you constructed a second unit on your lot,** how would one access it? If it's a corner lot or there's an alley running behind the property, access shouldn't be a problem. If there's 8 ft. to 10 ft. between houses, an access path between them probably won't impinge on anyone's privacy.

■ **Where are utility lines** (electricity, plumbing, gas) on your property? Are power lines overhead or underground?

■ **If your water is supplied by a well, where is it?** Likewise, if your house isn't served by a municipal sewer system, where is your septic tank and drain field?

DON'T FORGET ABOUT LANDSCAPING

It doesn't require a big budget to create a pleasant place to sit outdoors, a private pathway, or a sunny piece of yard that a tenant can "own." Landscaping is about optimizing natural beauty that's already there. If you're new to landscaping, here are two useful terms: *hardscape* refers to stone walls, brick walkways, fences, patios, and so on; *softscape* denotes plants.

Landscaping is a great way to define different living areas (as in "stake out your turf") and create private spaces that extend indoor living. One nice thing about using plants instead of fences, for example, is that even when planted in a straight line, plants aren't straight. Light breezes and sunlight make them flicker as they soften boundaries. Let pathways meander, too. You'll still get there but you'll have more fun along the way. Low-voltage path lights don't have to be super bright to increase safety, and they can meander, too. Whenever possible, use permeable hardscape materials so the softscape can get a drink when it rains. To screen parking areas, choose denser vegetation. And last (or maybe first), plant some things that are uselessly beautiful.

BELOW: This outdoor seating area adjoins a converted garage. Elevating the space makes it feel more private; plantings around a comfortable Adirondack chair make it cozy.

BOTTOM: Permeable pathways to an in-law unit can be beautiful, and they allow water to percolate into the earth.

Life has many agendas. We need beautiful places where we can just stare off into space and feed our souls.

SIX COMMON IN-LAWS

A successful in-law design must balance community-planning requirements, the needs of the homeowner and tenant, site conditions, and your budget. The type of in-law that's best for you will do the most to resolve these competing issues. Note that, in reality, in-laws are frequently hybrids of the six common types described in the following pages. That is, adding an in-law suite over

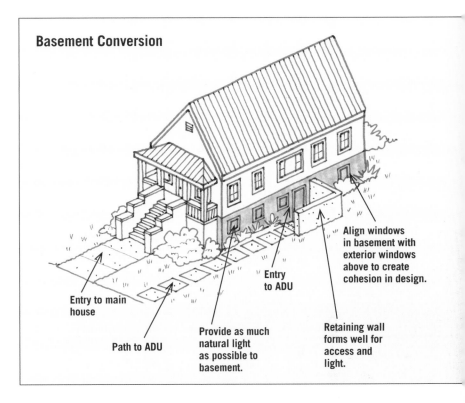

Basement Conversion

Align windows in basement with exterior windows above to create cohesion in design.

Entry to ADU

Entry to main house

Path to ADU

Provide as much natural light as possible to basement.

Retaining wall forms well for access and light.

BASEMENT CONVERSION
PROS
• Especially cost-effective if there's already enough headroom
• Can work well on a small lot with no place to add out or up
• On a sloping lot, the downhill side can accommodate a wall of windows
• There's ground-level access to yard, patio, and parking areas
• One-level living is a good setup for anyone with mobility problems
CONS
• Providing adequate natural light and ventilation can be challenging
• Blocking noise transmitted from the unit above can be costly
• If the basement has water problems, expensive drainage solutions may be required
• In urban areas, there may be privacy and security concerns
• Increasing headroom can be a major undertaking
• Meeting code requirements for emergency egress can be difficult

a garage is often similar to converting an attic, while converting the garage itself with its exposed studs and concrete floor is a lot like a basement conversion.

BASEMENT CONVERSIONS

One of the most cost-effective in-law conversions is one that is built in a basement. Correctly done, it is also one of the least expensive to heat and cool because temperatures will be moderated, to a degree, by its contact with the earth. The crux of a successful conversion is how un-basement-like you make it feel. In other words, it depends on how much sunlight, fresh air, comfort, and ceiling height you can get into the space.

Problems you might encounter There are many ways to correct water-related and structural problems that plague a basement and the foundation walls that surround it. Finding the most cost-effective one, however, is always the trick.

EVEN A DRY BASEMENT CAN SOMETIMES FLOOD, so wall-to-wall carpet and solid wood are poor flooring choices in that location. Instead, go with resilient flooring, tile, or stained concrete. Area rugs will lend color and warmth, and can be cleaned if they get wet.

Excessive moisture Although moisture can appear as condensation on the inside of basement walls and isn't a difficult thing to resolve, serious water problems have their source outside the basement. Thus, inexpensive interior "fixes" such as sump pumps or dehumidifiers will mitigate seasonal dampness to a degree, but living spaces may still smell musty and be plagued by mold. Increasing sunlight and ventilation is always welcome, but to keep moisture from entering, you'll need a solution that stops water before it gets through the basement walls.

By far the cheapest remedy—universally recommended by how-to books and ignored by homeowners—is to keep gutters and downspouts clear so they can direct water away from the foundation. Sloping the ground away from the house also helps, as does trimming back vegetation that hinders air circulation. Beyond that, cures get costly, such as installing perimeter drains around the house to remove the water or adding French drains uphill to intercept it. If you have running streams nearby, high ground-water levels, or if you live in a flood-prone district, developing the basement simply may not be viable.

Insufficient headroom For most codes, 7-ft. 6-in. finished ceilings are the minimum. If that's not what you have, you must either raise the house or lower the basement floor. Either approach is a big undertaking. Lowering the floor typically involves supporting the house, removing an existing slab, excavation, and augmenting or replacing all or part of the foundation and drainage system. Raising a house is a big project, too, but, in general, it's the better strategy because it creates more height for windows, and light that is more natural makes a basement feel less

BASEMENT EGRESS WINDOWS

To enable occupants to exit quickly in case of a fire, building codes require a method of escape—egress—for sleeping rooms on every level of the house, including the basement. Because egress windows must also be large enough to allow a fully equipped firefighter to enter, codes specify the size of the egress—typically, at least 20 in. wide and at least 24 in. tall, with a combined net-clear opening of at least 5.7 sq. ft.

To make it possible to climb out of an egress window, codes generally specify a maximum sill height of 44 in. above the floor, although a 32-in. sill height seems more reasonable if there are kids or elders present. (Check your local codes; some require two egress points for basement in-laws.) Installing an egress window in a concrete foundation wall is a job for a pro and may require the installation of an egress well.

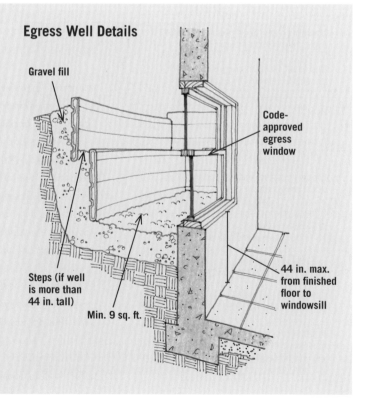

Egress Well Details

Gravel fill

Code-approved egress window

Steps (if well is more than 44 in. tall)

Min. 9 sq. ft.

44 in. max. from finished floor to windowsill

like a basement. If you also must replace a failing foundation (which requires supporting the house), then your choice is even clearer: Up she goes.

Lack of access (and escape) Two types of access can be difficult to provide in a basement in-law: emergency egress and entry. Some provision for emergency egress (escape) is required by code, and can be provided by a door that leads directly to the outside, or by a window that's large enough and low enough to crawl out of (see the sidebar on the facing page). An in-law unit's entry, on the other hand, could be through the house above, although, ideally, it should be an exterior door to maximize privacy for you and your tenant. If you have a large home, however, the door to the basement may be buried deep in the middle of the house. And your basement may have few or no windows.

Foundation problems If your foundation is failing and must be replaced, that's a great opportunity to create or upgrade a basement in-law. A structural engineer can assess the foundation and design its upgrade, but some common signs of foundation failure include large (½ in. or wider) vertical cracks through the foundation, foundation walls bowing in, sinking foundation corners, and flooring in the rooms above that crowns above a girder.

If your house is on a sloping lot, there's an interesting upside to enlarging the space under the house. The downhill face of a basement unit will be above ground so on that side, you can create a whole wall of windows. You may need to scoop out a lot of earth, build a retaining wall, and augment the foundation—all big undertakings—but the in-law unit that results will be sunny, spacious, and very un-basement-like.

Lack of natural light On a sloping lot, a good design can deliver abundant natural light into the unit. But if a

basement is buried under the house and is, say, two-thirds underground, natural light will be hard to come by. Frequently, homeowners add window wells. You can also try an interior solution such as sacrificing part of a closet upstairs to run a light tube to the roof. Your choice of artificial lighting matters, too: warm-fluorescent bulbs or dimmable halogen lighting can impart hues that are more natural. Lastly, if you share your yard or create a patio where tenants can catch some sun, those rays will help them lose the subterranean blues.

Other issues to consider Attending to a few details will increase the beauty and comfort of your basement in-law. So

You don't need large windows to make basement in-laws feel bright and cheery. Particularly in bathrooms, small windows do a better job of imparting light *and* privacy.

here are a few suggestions to help you keep cozy, defy gravity, hide the unsightly, suppress sounds, and provide nicer views from that subterranean lair.

Warm up Radiant floor heating can be a great choice for basement suites, whether heating loops are embedded in a concrete slab or installed beneath a finished floor (see the sidebar on p. 28). Radiant floors easily and evenly heat living spaces, and, in mild climates, they can help reduce condensation, especially in bathrooms.

Flush up Most of the time, wastes flow freely out of a house via downward-sloped drains. All it takes is gravity. If, however, you have a basement unit whose drainpipes are below the city sewer main, you'll need to pump wastes up to the main. This can be achieved by using a sewage ejection pump or a macerating toilet unit.

Sewage ejection pumps can be used with standard toilets. If the floor is concrete, you must first cut a slot in it and then excavate a trench large enough to accommodate drainpipes and a sewage-holding tank. (You can rent a concrete-cutting saw but it's a miserable DIY task; hire a concrete-cutting specialist instead.) In the bottom of the tank is a pump that propels sewage up to the sewer main via a 2-in. or 3-in. discharge pipe rising from the top of the tank.

A *macerating toilet unit* sits atop the floor and there's no need to cut a trench. The sewage goes directly from the toilet into a chamber whose cutting blades shred or grind the solids into a slurry that can be ejected through a much smaller discharge pipe—typically ¾ in. Macerating units cost more, but, once you factor in labor, they're competitively priced. Macerating units are less widely known, however, so check with building authorities to be sure these toilets are approved for your locale.

ADEQUATELY VENTING BATHS AND KITCHENS IS DOUBLY IMPORTANT in basement units because moisture vapor can condense on cool concrete walls. Put the bath fan on a 60-minute timer to be sure the moisture's gone. If summers are hot and humid, a dehumidifier will help, too.

A BETTER WAY TO INSULATE A BASEMENT

To retain conditioned air and prevent condensation on cool, below-grade basement walls, builders usually install 2-in.-thick rigid insulation over the walls, erect a stud wall on the inside, and then install drywall. The 6-in.-thick assembly eats up precious space. For that reason, companies such as Basement Systems® and Owens Corning® (see Appendix on p. 212) offer modular finishing systems that combine insulation, water-resistant panels, and the like. Installed by licensed professionals, such systems tend to be proprietary and pricey.

Homeowners determined to do their own basement conversions might want to look into the InSoFast® system (www.insofast.com). InSoFast insulation panels are 2 ft. by 4 ft. by 2-in.-thick extruded polystyrene (EPS) whose edges interlock so you can assemble wall sections on the ground, tilt them up, and adhere them to foundation walls using foam-board adhesive. Panels' backsides have vertical channels for moisture drainage and horizontal ones that you can feed electrical wiring through—later, if need be. On the panels' front sides are integral fastening strips that you can screw paperless drywall panels directly to, so you don't need to frame stud walls. The finished, insulated assembly is only 2½ in. thick.

GARAGE CONVERSIONS

Because garages are usually accessible, simply framed, and unfinished, they are among the easiest and most popular structures to convert to in-law units. Unlike basements or attics, there's generally little to undo before you can start renovating. When the framing is exposed, there are relatively few surprises. Consequently, many types of garage conversions exist. To simplify things, we'll focus on converting a garage *shell*; that is, the ground floor of a one- or two-car detached garage. In "Garage Hybrids," (see p. 29), we'll briefly consider three other types of conversions: over-garage units, detached garages with add-on living spaces, and attached garages.

Problems you might encounter Garages are so simply built that structural issues are rarely an impediment to doing what you want. More likely, the chief obstacle will be satisfying local parking requirements. You may have to replace parking places lost by the conversion.

Lack of parking If local codes are relaxed, parking cars behind each other in the driveway (tandem parking) may suffice. In other instances, you may be required to pave part of the yard to create new parking places. Where codes are more stringent, you may have to erect a covered or enclosed parking area. Moreover, if your lot is not large enough to accommodate a replacement parking solution, you'll have to seek a variance or abandon your plans to convert the garage.

Irregular or failing floors If garage floors are crumbling or buckled and not reinforced with steel, tear them out, then rough-in new plumbing and other utilities, pour a new slab and, if necessary, a new foundation. If the floor is reasonably flat and stable (small surface cracks are acceptable), install a vapor barrier and pour a new topping slab over it. Garage floors are often sloped to shed water

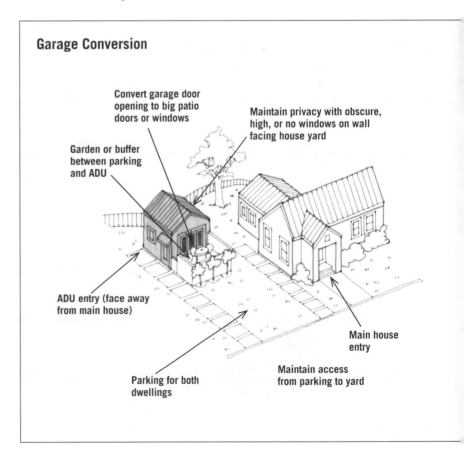

Garage Conversion

Convert garage door opening to big patio doors or windows

Maintain privacy with obscure, high, or no windows on wall facing house yard

Garden or buffer between parking and ADU

ADU entry (face away from main house)

Main house entry

Parking for both dwellings

Maintain access from parking to yard

The over-garage unit at left has privacy, accessibility, and great views of the Oregon countryside.

toward the garage doors, so the topping slab often levels the floor as well. If the finish floor will be tiled, a self-leveling underlayment concrete, which evens out irregularities, offers another solution.

Other issues to consider   There are so many possible configurations of garage conversions that it's hard to identify any single issue that stands out as more problematic than others. But along with the ones noted above, you'll want to consider the following early in the design and planning process.

Utility hookups   Getting electricity, gas, water, and sewage lines to a detached garage is rarely a big problem. It depends on how far the garage is from street hookups. But if there is a lot of concrete or asphalt to cut through, you can hire a concrete-cutting specialist to cut a utilities trench in short order.

Low-down garages   If the garage floor is below the level of the city sewer main, plumbing fixtures installed in the unit will need a special pump to raise sewage and gray water to the sewer main (see p. 26).

RADIANT FLOORS, TOASTY TENANTS

More and more garage conversions include radiant heating when there's a new concrete floor to be poured. It's easy to see why. PEX radiant tubing is field-proven, easy to work with, and the pairing of PEX and concrete creates a formidable thermal mass that provides comfortable heat without blowing air around. Better yet, if you install windows on south-facing walls, the slab will absorb sunlight and radiate it back. If you prefer wood floors, you can still have radiant heating. Manufactured heating panels can be easily installed before the finish floor goes down. You won't have the benefit of concrete's thermal mass, but the heat will still delight bare feet.

Radiant Floor

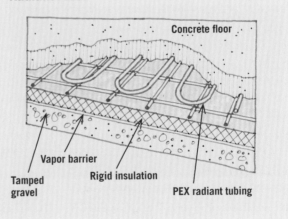

Concrete floor

Vapor barrier

Rigid insulation

Tamped gravel

PEX radiant tubing

GARAGE CONVERSION

PROS

- Good solution if the lot is small and a basement conversion isn't viable

- Economical way to renovate an existing structure whose framing is exposed

- Access to natural light and ventilation is usually good

- Detached garage conversion offers privacy, sound separation

- Attached garage conversion allows elderly relative or caregiver to be close by

- Entry and egress is typically easy to provide

CONS

- May have to create additional parking spaces to satisfy code

- Garages are sometimes underbuilt, and may need structural reinforcement

- Garage floors are often sloped, and may be in bad repair

- Drainage and dampness problems are common

- Health and safety concerns if petrochemical smells or residue are present

WOOD OVER CONCRETE

Wood floors add class to a garage conversion, but they must be carefully detailed to keep moisture from wicking through concrete and warping them. A vapor barrier and a layer of insulation help keep wood stable. In floating floor systems, the barrier is often a thin layer of foam, topped by engineered wood flooring that is relatively stable. You can place these systems over self-leveling underlayment concrete.

If you want the spring and warmth of solid wood flooring, however, it's best to install it over a grid of *sleepers* and a plastic film vapor barrier (see below). Place rigid insulation between the sleepers. If the existing concrete floor slopes, you'll need to taper the sleepers or shim them to level.

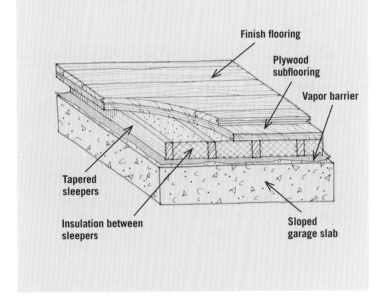

Finish flooring

Plywood subflooring

Vapor barrier

Tapered sleepers

Insulation between sleepers

Sloped garage slab

Rotted studs, failed foundations
Garages are often modest constructions whose foundations were afterthoughts. So sills, stud bottoms, and the lowest siding courses must often be replaced, along with a cracked or crumbling foundation. It might be tempting just to tear the whole thing down and start over. Don't do it. Or at least don't do it until you've had a chance to review local codes and perhaps research your property. Your ability to convert the garage may depend on whether it has *grandfather status* (see the sidebar on p. 10). Two of the in-laws in this book were possible only because their original structures were grandfathered in (see p. 183 and p. 188). Had they torn down the structures, they may have lost the chance to convert!

GARAGE HYBRIDS
Sometimes garage units combine features of several different in-law types, so read the other sections to which they relate. Because over-garage and garage bump-out units physically connect to active garages, fire codes require that firewalls separate the differing uses (see the sidebar on p. 30).

Over-garage unit   If you want to create an in-law unit by adding a second story to a garage, consult a structural engineer.

FIREWALL SAFETY

Whenever living spaces adjoin a garage, fire codes require "use separation" between the two areas. Use separation can sometimes be achieved by installing two layers of ⅝-in. Type X drywall over the garage-side of the shared wall (or ceiling). However, always check local fire codes to see what fire rating they require for such firewalls. For example, a 1-hr.-rated firewall is intended to slow the spread of fire from one side to the other for a period of at least one hour.

With plenty of natural light and privacy, this over-garage unit has the best features of an attic conversion and a detached cottage.

Likewise, if the space over the garage was intended only for storage—not people—the existing foundation may not be large enough to support the live loads of someone living upstairs. But if the garage was built with a potential live-in space above it (see p. 125 and the photo below), the foundation may be adequate. If the unit's floors are springy, it may be possible to add a girder and support posts underneath to shorten the span of the floor joists without affecting the garage's functionality.

Garage bump-out A commodious in-law apartment can often be created by annexing part of a garage and adding a bump-out

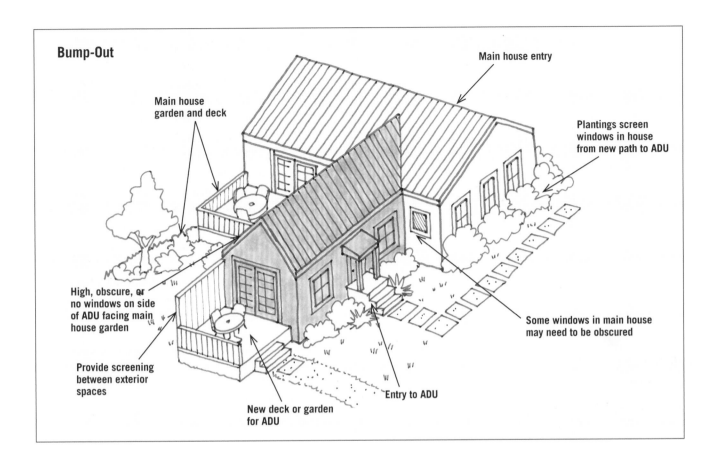

Bump-Out

Main house entry

Main house garden and deck

Plantings screen windows in house from new path to ADU

High, obscure, or no windows on side of ADU facing main house garden

Some windows in main house may need to be obscured

Provide screening between exterior spaces

Entry to ADU

New deck or garden for ADU

(see p. 68, for example). It's essentially the same as bumping out from a house (see "Bump-Outs," right). If your lot has enough room for a garage bump-out, this arrangement offers privacy and separation from the house without sacrificing garage parking spaces.

Converting an attached garage This conversion is essentially the same as that of a detached garage, except that attached garages tend to be newer, more solidly built, and finished to a greater degree. Because attached garages share a wall with the house, noise and privacy are the big issues. If the garage was built according to code, that shared wall will probably be a double-layered firewall, which may be easiest to soundproof from the house side. Locating a front door for the new unit may also take some head scratching: Ideally, it should be on an exterior wall far from the shared wall so

people in the house won't hear the tenant coming and going.

BUMP-OUTS

A bump-out (a small addition to a house), is a popular way to create an in-law unit that conserves lot-space and building materials. Because it bumps right against the house, there's one less wall to construct; more ambitious bump-out units may even annex several rooms of the house. But they can be tricky to design. Being so close, a bump-out can impact the sunlight, usable space, and privacy of the house—and that of neighboring houses. So hiring an architect to design your bump-out might be money well spent.

Problems you might encounter

Constructing an addition is straight-forward, so the things most likely to complicate a bump-out project will be code-related.

BUMP-OUT

PROS

- It doesn't take up much space

- Cost-effective because walls are shared with existing structure

- Makes it easy to create a court-yard that increases privacy and screens views

- Elderly parent or caregiver can be close by

- Viable option if house is too small for carve-out unit

CONS

- Adding a bump-out may make the main house look too big, crowd neighbors, block light

- May conflict with scale of neighborhood

- Privacy and sound issues between house and unit

- Fewer people will want to rent a unit that's so close to the main house and the landlord/lady

IF THE KITCHEN AND BATHROOM OF AN IN-LAW UNIT ARE FAR FROM THE HOUSE, installing an on-demand water heater close to the unit's fixtures makes sense. Pipe runs will be shorter than tying into the house water heater, and less heat will be lost in transmission.

Zoning issues The primary issue will be the size of your lot and the percentage of it that may be covered by structures. Typically, the combined square footage of the house and the in-law unit must not exceed 30% or 40% of the total lot area. (Patios and outside decks are usually not included in the calculations, but check local zoning or building codes to be sure.)

Another issue likely to come into play will be *setbacks* (minimum distances to property lines); particularly if the house was constructed before current codes were adopted. That is, though house setbacks from property lines may not conform to current codes, additions *must* conform to current codes including, among others, setbacks and height restrictions. Their intent is to keep new structures from adversely impacting neighbors.

Getting the scale right Another issue, *massing*, though not usually addressed by codes, may also affect neighbors. Massing has more to do with courtesy and common sense than law. If your lot is exceptionally narrow, for example, codes may allow you to add a bump-out to your house, but the mass of the combined structures may disturb the rhythm of adjoining yards and houses or seriously impinge your neighbor's privacy and peace of mind. If you can keep the peace by, say, building an in-law cottage at the back of your lot instead, that's probably a wise move. A good neighbor is a pearl beyond price.

Other issues to consider Any well-designed second unit responds to the specifics of a situation, including the site, the house's layout, and the needs of the homeowner and tenant. Because bump-outs attach to the house, they influence its floor plan to a greater degree than most other types of in-laws.

Locating the addition In general, a single-story addition will be the least disruptive to neighbors and the functioning of the main house. Follow the contour of the land, if possible. If the lot is

TYING IN THE ADDITION

The bump-out should look like it belongs to the house, and there are several ways to tie the buildings together. Structurally, the bump-out's foundation should be "pinned" to the house's with rebar and epoxy; exterior drains should tie in to the house's perimeter drains; and the roof should be carefully flashed to the house roof or siding to keep water out.

Visually, matching exterior elements is key. The two structures should have roughly the same proportions. Using similar roof pitches, exterior trim, siding, window and door styles, and paint helps both sections look like one house.

flat, continuing the floor level of the house into the addition will create spaces that all ages can easily navigate. If the lot slopes, putting the bump-out slightly lower may create more interesting spaces and get more light into sun-starved rooms. Ideally, your bump-out design will enhance the house in some way, perhaps by creating a courtyard or an "L" that blocks an undesirable view or offers privacy from a neighboring property.

Optimizing sunlight   Where the bump-out abuts the house, it may block a door or window, requiring a change in traffic flow and some way to get more light into the room. (If the affected room is a bedroom, keep in mind that fire codes require an egress as well; see p. 25.) The most obvious solution is to get sunlight by adding or enlarging a window on another wall, adding a skylight, or opening up the house floor plan so that light from other rooms can enter. If the lot slopes and the bump-out addition is slightly lower, you might also add clerestory windows high on the shared wall.

Weighing layouts   Finding a workable floor plan is often a balance of how easily and affordably you can build it vs. what best suits the occupant. If there's a bath or kitchen on the house side of a shared wall, it makes sense to put the in-law unit's bath or kitchen on the other side. The plumbing is already there: just open the wall and make connections. Such a setup also puts similar functions back to back, generally a good idea because noise and activity levels will coincide at the same time of day.

The other variable, what suits the occupant, is a bit more elusive. If you're building the bump-out for an elderly parent or a caregiver, you might want his or her bedroom close to the house so it's easy for you to drop in for a chat or respond quickly if there's a mishap. On the other hand, if your tenant is an adult child or a renter, privacy may trump access. In that case, place the unit's entrance and active areas far from the house. This distance is also advisable if your tenant keeps odd hours—especially true of young adults.

While we're on the topic of privacy, keep neighbors in mind, too. Place windows high up on any wall that's close to a property line or faces a neighbor's bedroom or bath. Planting living screens between houses and along access paths also helps.

Managing utilities   It probably isn't worth adding a separate electric meter for a bump-out, especially if the unit incorporates rooms from the house. Instead, note average monthly bills before and after the unit is rented, then charge your tenant a fixed monthly sum based on the difference in energy consumption, plus a small fee against future costs such as repairing or replacing appliances.

CARVE-OUTS

A carve-out is an in-law unit created by transforming a few existing rooms in a house into separate quarters. It is the quickest and most economical in-law to complete because there is little construction involved. In fact, creating a carve-out is more about social engineering than structural engineering. In other words, it's about figuring out how to transform unused rooms into comfortable (if compact) living quarters while maintaining privacy for everyone.

When carve-outs work best   Because carve-outs are the most spatially intimate living arrangement of any in-law type, they can be the most challenging. A carve-out might be a good choice when:

■ **Your house has become too big for you** but for various reasons (your mortgage is paid off, your taxes are low, you love the neighborhood) you don't want to move.

DOORS HAVE EARS. If soundproofing between living units matters, remove doors in shared walls, frame and fill the opening with insulation, and cover it with drywall. Interior doors are typically only 1⅜ in. thick, so some sound goes right through them.

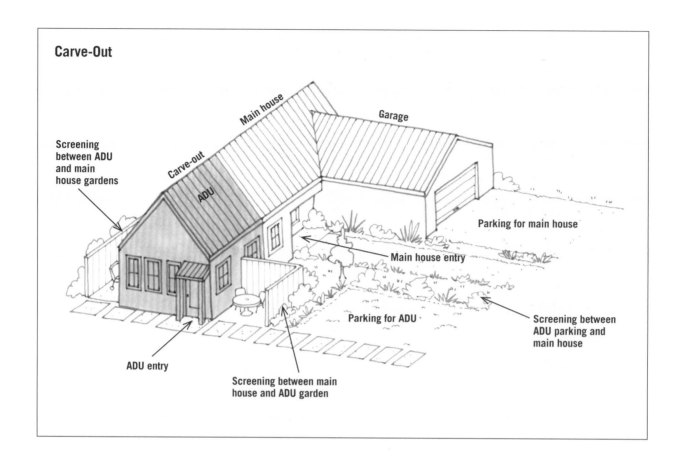

Carve-Out

Screening between ADU and main house gardens

Main house

Carve-out

ADU

Garage

Parking for main house

Main house entry

Parking for ADU

ADU entry

Screening between main house and ADU garden

Screening between ADU parking and main house

- **The site is too small to bump out,** converting the basement isn't viable, there's no attic to develop, or the garage can't be converted.
- **An adult child or elderly parent or** caregiver is coming to live with you or you need a nanny, nurse, or caregiver close by, full-time.
- **You need to create an in-law unit** quickly in response to some sudden life change affecting you or a family member.
- **You need to create a** unit economically.

Problems you might encounter Grouping rooms with similar functions along a shared wall can also lead to more cost-effective solutions. Plumbing, for example, can be very disruptive if long pipe runs are required.

CARVE-OUT

PROS

- Least expensive conversion
- Makes use of unused rooms
- Well suited for relative, friend, or someone you want close by
- Requires no land, so it's a good solution for a small lot

CONS

- Sound and privacy issues because of shared walls
- Separating utilities can be tricky
- Not the best layout if you must rent to strangers

Difficult room placement Kitchens and bathrooms are the trickiest rooms to position because they are the most complex, requiring plumbing and wiring hookups and, in some cases, structural modifications to support, say, a tub or toilet. If possible, put the in-law unit's kitchen back to back with the house kitchen.

Likewise, locate the unit's bathroom on a shared "wet wall" to shorten pipe runs and simplify drain and vent stack connections. Keep in mind that baths and kitchens need vent fans, too, so anticipate where to run vent ducts. Lastly, put bedrooms in the quietest part of the suite—often, the room farthest from the street.

Sound travels easily Even if the person on the other side of the wall is

STRATEGIES FOR CLOSE QUARTERS

Put "like near like" when devising a layout for your carve-out unit. Try to put quiet rooms in the in-law unit near quiet rooms in the house, and active rooms near active rooms. By doing so, you'll be less likely to disturb each other because you'll be doing the same activities—whether cooking or sleeping—at the same times of day. If you'll be renting the carve-out unit, "like near like" is also a good principle to apply when choosing a tenant: choose someone whose lifestyle is similar to yours and your habits will be less likely to conflict in close quarters. Ideally, that person would be a friend or someone you hear about through your social network.

A shared wall between a bedroom and a dining room is far more peaceful than a bedroom-kitchen pair-up.

WHEN SOUND-PROOFING, give a thought to light sealing, too. Especially in bedrooms, light entering from the other living area can disturb someone trying to sleep. Weather-stripping the perimeter of a shared door or installing heavy curtains may do the trick.

quiet, the incidental noises of living can be distracting because they are unexpected. So don't scrimp on soundproofing. Short-term, you can separate living areas by locking doors but for long-term comfort and privacy, remove interior doors in shared walls, frame-in the openings and then insulate and cover the framing with drywall. (This assumes, of course, that the tenant doesn't need quick access to the house—or vice versa.)

Creating a new entrance If you must add a new exterior door to maintain privacy, here are a few tips. Note what local codes say on the subject; many don't allow house and second-unit entries on the same wall. For maximal privacy, locate the in-law's new entrance on a sidewall and screen it with vegetation. Your tenant will also appreciate a modest porch or overhang that will block snow or rain as she roots for her keys. Don't forget a light, either.

Other issues to consider How easily you convert house rooms into a carve-out suite depends in large part on what's already there. Choosing a suite of rooms that includes a bathroom will expedite the conversion and keep costs down. So will resolving the following issues:

Parking It's often a sore point with neighbors, so resolve it if you can. The solution may be as simple as widening your drive slightly so the tenant can park in tandem.

Sharing resources Figure a fair way to divide utilities; installing a separate meter is impractical. And share laundry facilities if they can be accessed in some way that preserves privacy and separation of space.

Providing access If possible, create a foyer inside the main entrance, with entry doors to each living unit; you'll be spared the considerable cost of adding a separate exterior door.

ATTIC CONVERSIONS

Many people assume that an attic is "free space" just because it's there, but the reality is usually more complicated. Attic framing is often skeletal, strong enough to support a roof and to provide a ceiling for the rooms below, but not really stout enough to support the live loads of someone living in the attic. Consequently, how easily and affordably you can convert your attic depends on the answers to these questions:

- **Is there enough headroom** to satisfy local codes? (Most require 7 ft. 6 in.)
- **Are attic floor joists strong enough** to support a living space?
- **Is the attic presently accessible** via code-approved stairs and a separate exterior entrance?

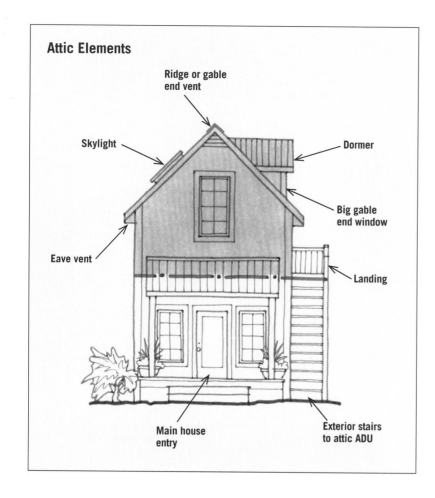

Attic Elements

Ridge or gable end vent

Skylight

Dormer

Big gable end window

Eave vent

Landing

Main house entry

Exterior stairs to attic ADU

ATTIC CONVERSION

PROS

- Space-conserving choice, appropriate for a small lot

- If there is adequate headroom, conversion may be economical

- If enough windows and skylights, can feel light-filled and spacious

- Well-suited to adult child living at home, younger renter

CONS

- Can be the most expensive and complicated in-law to build

- Noise can bother people living downstairs

- Codes may require second egress

- Stairs are difficult for older people or those with mobility problems

- It can be difficult to provide adequate heating, cooling, and ventilation

Can enough insulation, ventilation, or air-conditioning be added to make the space habitable? In hot climates, this question is particularly important.

Problems you might encounter If you answered "no" to any of these questions, you should speak to an architect. Correcting any of these conditions will require a well-thought-out design and modifications to the structure. An architect will know structural engineers and other specialists who can help get the job done right.

Lack of headroom Beneath sloping rafters, ceiling height is greatest under the ridge of the roof and decreases as you approach the eaves. Generally, adequate headroom means having enough height to walk through living spaces and to

use various functional areas—kitchen, bathroom, stairs, and so on—without bumping your head or having to stoop. It's acceptable for closets, storage areas, and, say, ceilings over beds to be less than full height—in fact, those are good uses of marginal spaces.

But if the attic's headroom is inadequate, generally you'll need to reframe some part of the roof to create additional height. Adding a gable dormer or a shed dormer is a common way to gain a little headroom and provide a wall for windows. If, however, you can't create enough headroom by installing dormers, raising or reframing the whole roof may be the next option. It's a hugely expensive one that may involve structural modifications all the way down to the foundation. Unless you have a compelling reason to convert

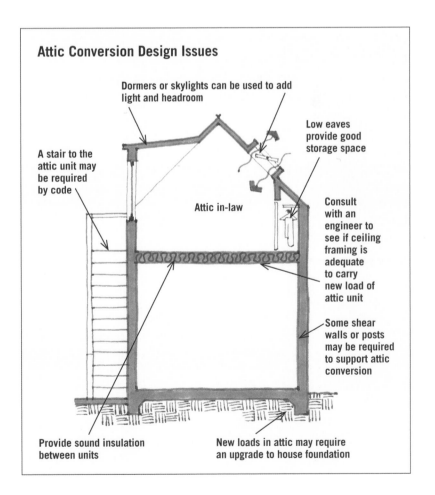

Attic Conversion Design Issues

Dormers or skylights can be used to add light and headroom

Low eaves provide good storage space

A stair to the attic unit may be required by code

Attic in-law

Consult with an engineer to see if ceiling framing is adequate to carry new load of attic unit

Some shear walls or posts may be required to support attic conversion

Provide sound insulation between units

New loads in attic may require an upgrade to house foundation

the attic in this case, consider some other way to create an in-law unit.

Inadequate floor joists If floors are springy and joists are undersized, you will need to reinforce them. Here again, solutions quickly become complicated and costly: get advice from an architect or an experienced general contractor. If joists are adequately sized but floors are springy, adding a ¾-in. plywood subfloor may stiffen things up.

If joists are inadequate, nailing or bolting additional joists to the old ones—a procedure called "sistering"—may suffice. Because larger joists are also deeper, how-ever, sistering may not be viable in an attic with limited headroom. Bolting metal flitch plates to joists (see the sidebar on p. 204) is another option, but one best left to a pro.

If reinforcing joists is out, your next recourse is to shorten the distance that the joists must span by adding a girder or a bearing wall underneath. Typically, this option is disruptive to rooms below the attic and requires some modification of the foundation.

Lack of access Providing safe access to an attic suite depends on where the stairs are located, what condition they're in, and what local codes require. Stairs take up a lot of space and impact privacy because no one likes the sound of footfalls overhead. So it's best if they don't run through the middle of downstairs living spaces. For this reason, stairs for attic rental units are often located toward one end of a house.

Local codes may require a second egress location for attic units, usually a set of exterior stairs, and they tend to be unattractive. If you want to locate them on the side of your house, make sure you have enough room to access them—and your neighbor's consent. Stairs are large and generally ungainly and anyone using them could potentially look down into a neighbor's windows.

IF THE HOUSE IS SERVED BY A FORCED-AIR HEATING SYSTEM or a hydronic system, have an HVAC specialist assess the system's capacity and determine if it can be extended to the attic. In many cases, homeowners just install electric baseboard heaters in an attic unit, though a licensed electrician should first assess the house capacity— and do the installation.

Cost-effective climate control
Options abound for controlling air temperature and quality in an attic, but the best ones moderate temperatures without consuming energy. Windows and skylights that open, for example, allow warm, moist air to rise and exit; more windows equal better cross-ventilation. An adequately insulated roof, in turn, will conserve conditioned air and prevent excessive heat build-up in summer. Air allowed to flow freely under the roof sheathing, entering at soffit vents, rising as it heats, and exiting at ridge or gable-end vents, will also help to keep the attic cool.

Adequate insulation and natural ventilation require rafters deep enough to accommodate them. A properly sized rafter allows air coming up from eaves to flow over insulation (and under the roof sheathing) and to exit at ridge or gable-end vents. If your rafters aren't deep enough, there is a plethora of choices, but they tend to be costly to implement or operate. Reframing the roof with larger rafters or installing rigid insulation atop the roof sheathing cost a lot up front. Consequently, homeowners usually opt for mechanical solutions such as conditioners and vent fans.

Other issues to consider If you can find workable solutions to the major problems, you're on your way to creating an in-law suite in the attic. Attending to a few more issues will enhance the comfort and privacy of you and your tenant.

Sound control This is particularly important to whoever lives below the attic. Look at "Soundproofing a Ceiling" (p. 47) for an optimal way to lessen sound transmission through floors, have a look at the real-life solutions on p. 44 and p. 202, and continue your research online. As you'll see, there are varying opinions about the most cost-effective ways to suppress sound.

If the attic is unfinished and floorboards can be easily pulled up, insulate between joists to muffle sounds, and then install a carpet pad and carpeting. Many pros think that a pad and carpet are at least as important as acoustic insulation. In kitchens and bathrooms where carpet isn't appropriate, put foam underlayment over the subfloor, then install resilient flooring such as vinyl or Marmoleum®.

Plumbing routes When converting an attic, note the location and condition of existing plumbing pipes, and repair or upgrade them if necessary. If the pipes are serviceable, you'll be able to connect to ones nearby, thus conserving materials and space. Drainpipes for plumbing fixtures can be tricky to route because they're large and must slope so wastes can drain freely—another instance where adequately sized joists will make the job easier. To suppress the sounds of flushing toilets and running water, nothing beats cast-iron DWV pipes; in fact, they may be required by local codes.

A place in the sun If a small lot was a big reason for creating an attic unit, there may not be much yard to share with a tenant. In that case, consider adding a roof deck. This is most easily achieved if there's already a flat-roofed addition to support the deck, as there was with the Holmses' house (see p. 208). Another alternative is a let-in deck, which is virtually invisible from the street but requires the highest level of skill to frame, flash, and finish correctly in order to prevent water from leaking into living areas below the deck.

IN-LAW COTTAGES

Every architectural project has constraints or issues that affect its design. Freestanding in-laws such as cottages

COTTAGE (STAND-ALONE)
PROS
• Easy to locate on a large lot, especially if there's an alley at the back
• Offers best privacy, sound separation, and the most elbow room
• Ideal for independent elder or adult child at home, and a very desirable rental unit
• Greatest number of design options
• If neighboring houses are close, the unit can usually be sited so it won't block the sun
• Providing a separate utility meter is easy
CONS
• Moderately expensive to construct an entire new building
• Reduces open yard space
• If the unit is far from the street, a long access path may be required
• May require long utility runs to reach the unit

are no exception. They may not face the headroom or sunlight issues of, say, a basement conversion or a bump-out, but clever design solutions for cottages often spring from balancing competing claims, starting with planning constraints.

Problems you might encounter Much as all of us love to groan about restrictions, they can help us focus on what's doable. They create a framework, if you will, in which to structure our ideas.

Code requirements This is the most restrictive issue to consider, particularly codes regarding maximum allowable size, setbacks from property lines, and height. Grandfathered cottages (see p. 10) needn't conform to existing codes if properly

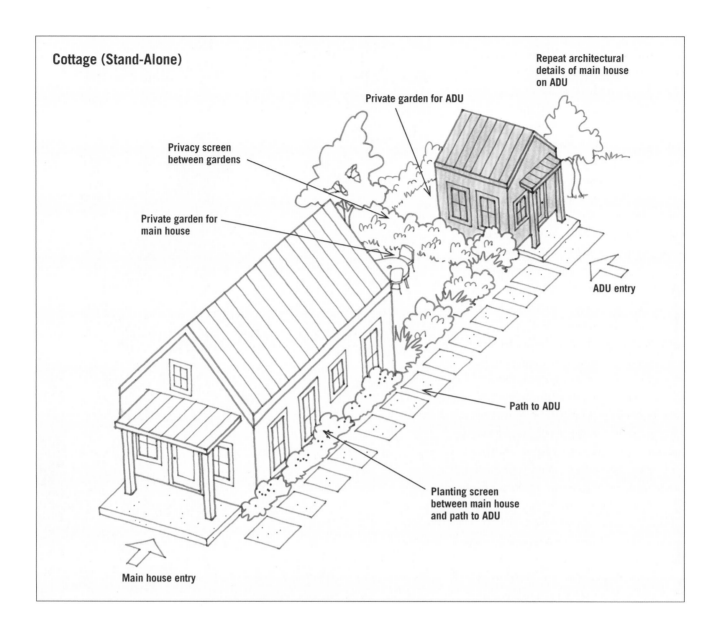

Cottage (Stand-Alone)

Repeat architectural details of main house on ADU

Private garden for ADU

Privacy screen between gardens

Private garden for main house

ADU entry

Path to ADU

Planting screen between main house and path to ADU

Main house entry

permitted and constructed before codes were enacted. However, significantly remodeling them may trigger design reviews. Check local codes to be sure.

Providing parking This can be a thorny problem to solve. First, is there room to create a parking space for tenants and, if so, will it be close enough to a cottage in the back of your yard? If there's an alley or side street across the back of your property, that will help.

Expensive utility connections It can be costly to dig a long trench to extend drains and utilities to the cottage. It gets even more expensive if you have to cut through asphalt or concrete, or route the utilities around a big tree or an existing patio.

Expensive site preparation If your site is completely flat or has standing water during the rainy season, you may need to install an extensive drainage system. Indeed, site conditions may decide the type of foundation you choose, whether a slab on a dry site or raised footings on a wet one. You might also choose to grade the site to create a berm that visually separates the cottage from the house or an earth ramp (see p. 94) for older tenants with mobility issues.

Other things to consider Getting a cottage to fit right on-site without diminishing the privacy of neighbors is sometimes a challenge, though less so if you have a large or rural lot.

Siting the structure Siting a cottage is often a trade-off between privacy and access. If the person living in the cottage is an older parent with limited mobility, locating the cottage nearer to the house (and to parking) makes sense. A cottage located in the back of the property, far from the street, may be too far to walk. On the other hand, an adult child, a renter, or an older person in good health may prefer greater privacy and distance from the house.

Site conditions include solar access, views, how close neighboring properties are, how close parking spots are, and so on. As cities become denser, their codes address these issues—limiting, for example, the degree that an addition can shade a neighboring property.

Other important factors include the presence of large or historic trees, which, increasingly, are protected by city regulations. Typically, you can't build within the drip line of a protected tree, which further limits where you can locate a cottage. Thus, a tree sometimes becomes an important part of the design (see the sidebar on p. 176). When siting, remember to allocate enough space so that the cottage also has a little yard of its own or a private patio.

CREATING ACCESSIBILITY FOR ALL AGES

Whatever the type, many in-laws are created to care for an aging parent or a disabled relative, or to anticipate home-owners' needs as they grow older. It will

This backyard cottage in Eugene, Oregon, achieves a lot in 269 sq. ft. To the east, a sleeping loft rests above the kitchen; to the west, the bathroom abuts a utility closet. In between there's a large studio space. Add lots of glass and the result is light, roomy, and pleasant.

AS PEOPLE AGE, their vision often declines and it takes longer for their eyes to focus when moving between bright and dimly lit areas. Consequently, provide more light (inside and out) around entries to avoid falls.

come as no surprise to anyone over 50 that as we age, our physical abilities gradually ratchet down. Each year those stairs get a little steeper.

Over the years, housing designers have become more aware of the needs of people with reduced capacities—as evidenced by all the terms used to describe housing that is more accessible (see the sidebar below). Whatever the labels, the fact remains that designs and products that are friendly to people with limited abilities are also easier to use by able-bodied people. At any age, human abilities are a continuum of varying strength, mobility, range of motion, dexterity, balance, hearing, and vision. A well-designed home will be accessible to people of all ages and abilities, and that's especially true of in-law units where small spaces often have multiple uses.

RAMPS AND APPROACHES

To create the most accessible entrance to an in-law unit, eliminate steps: They hinder both an elder using a walker and a parent pushing a stroller. In place of steps, provide a sloping approach—either by landscaping

or by building a ramp. If the unit's main entrance is no more than 18 in. above grade (ground level), landscaping a gradual, sloping path to the front door is preferable to a ramp. It will cost less and look better (see the photo on the facing page).

If the entrance is 18 in. to 30 in. above grade, construct a ramp. Per code, ramps can be no steeper than a 1-in-12 slope, but that's still very steep to a person in a wheelchair. A 1-in-20 slope is much easier, though the gentler the slope, the more space a ramp will require. (Note: A 1-in-20 slope is the maximum allowable without requiring the installation of a handrail. A 1-in-20 slope rises 1 ft. vertically for each 20 ft. traveled horizontally.) It takes great skill to integrate a ramp into a home's exterior and have it look good, so if your in-law unit needs one, consult an architect experienced with ADA issues. If the elevation change is more than 30 in., consider installing a mechanical lift. For a more extensive discussion of accessibility requirements for your in-law unit, see p. 212 in the Appendix.

THE LANGUAGE OF ACCESSIBILITY

If you're exploring ways to make your in-law unit easier to access and use, you'll come across certain phrases repeatedly. Here's what they mean:

Accessible design: This is housing that's designed to be accessible to and usable by everyone, regardless of his or her age or physical condition. Wider than usual doors and halls, doorways without thresholds, and ramps rather than steps are examples of design features. Accessible design also applies to handles, switches, and other products used within a home.

Universal design: Think accessible design with a long view. Universal design tries to create living spaces that meet present needs and adapt easily to future ones. Thus, an in-law unit built according to universal design principles might have an unfinished

area plumbed and wired for a future kitchen, or bathroom walls framed to support future grab bars, or an exterior wall framed to make it easier to add an addition when more space is needed. Also called *flex housing*.

ADA-compliant: In 1990, the Americans with Disabilities Act (ADA) became law with the intent to reduce physical barriers so that everyone could enjoy equal access to workplaces and public facilities. The phrase "ADA-compliant" means that a structure meets all the strict regulations of the law. This milestone legislation also accelerated accessible residential design, though it doesn't cover single-family homes per se. So if you hear someone describe a single-family home as ADA-compliant, what they mean is more accurately "ADA-inspired."

Thoughtful interior
features improve
accessibility, but no
less important are
exterior features
such as gently
sloped, slip-resistant
pathways.

from gloom to glory

Whenever Larry and Ann Tramutola peered into their basement, they saw only wasted space, a black hole so cavernous and dank that anything stored in it would be moldy in a month. So they invited architect Jon Larson over to see what could be done with it. Larson loves a challenge.

By repositioning the stairs, removing the carport, resurfacing the parking area, and erecting a screen (eventually to be covered with vegetation), the architect created a sunny patio without sacrificing any parking spaces.

The back of the house, before. Badly located stairs and a covered parking area blocked sunlight and limited access to the basement.

He first considered the site, which sloped steeply away from the street. The front of the house, a single-story Craftsman bungalow, was at grade level, but, in the back, its floor was roughly 10 ft. above grade. The house was built on one side of a gully, which allowed water to pool against the foundation and made the basement unusable. That meant big outlays for drainage and sewer issues even before remodeling could begin.

In addition, the surrounding structures made the site dark. Most of the buildings on adjacent lots were higher, and a carport next to the back stairs blocked even more light. To make the basement even darker and more constricted, the stairs came right down the middle of the building. Amid the gloom, however, Larson saw dazzling possibilities.

THE IN-LAW TAKES SHAPE

If, for starters, you demolished the parking structure and moved the stairs far to the right—ideally, all the way to the setback line—you'd have room for an outdoor patio. And with the east wall of the basement now open to the

WHENEVER YOU OPEN UP A SHARED WALL OR A CEILING that gives access to a floor above, that's a great time to make changes to the main house. It will never be easier to add a supply pipe, replace an outdated drain, insulate for sound, or run wire to a new electrical outlet.

Floor Plan

Chimney mass removed to create closet

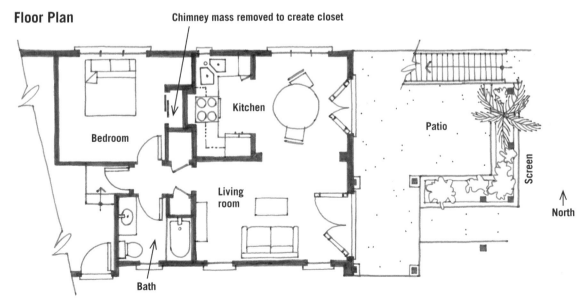

Bedroom

Kitchen

Living room

Bath

Patio

Screen

↑ North

Two sets of 8-ft.-tall French doors create an indoor-outdoor patio in which light, air, and people can move freely. With its generous overhang, the patio is a great place to entertain, whatever the weather.

morning sun, you could install double sets of 8-ft.-high French doors. (The basement had 9-ft.-plus ceilings.) Doors that tall would allow sunlight to penetrate deep into the space. And so it went. The farther he imagined light reaching into the dark, the more Larson saw.

Shortly, Larson showed Ann and Larry sketches of an elegant in-law apartment. They could rent it, use it as an office, put up relatives, or house one of their kids. It would be a big undertaking—rebuilding the basement and upgrading the drainage were big-ticket items. But the property had appreciated nicely since they bought it 30 years earlier and, besides, they were committed to staying in the community. So they decided to create an in-law they'd want to live in.

IMPROVING LIFE UPSTAIRS

Developing the basement also improved the rooms upstairs. Moving the exterior stairs to one side gave the upper deck greater privacy and more usable space. Dining al fresco became a pleasure. Reframing the basement ceiling proved a good time to replace the bungalow's 80-year-old plumbing. And once the basement ceiling was soundproofed, the upstairs floors were warmer and more comfortable than they had ever been.

SOUNDPROOFING A CEILING

To block sound, you have to be meticulous about construction details. The two drywall layers forming the ceiling were screwed to resilient channels instead of being attached directly to the joists. This, in effect, allows them to "float." But the real key to interrupting the transmission of sound is cutting the ceiling drywall ¼ in. to ½ in. short of the walls all the way around, and then filling the gap with acoustical sealant.

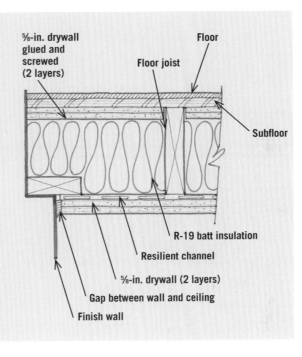

⅝-in. drywall glued and screwed (2 layers)

Floor

Floor joist

Subfloor

R-19 batt insulation

Resilient channel

⅝-in. drywall (2 layers)

Gap between wall and ceiling

Finish wall

Though the trim was inspired by Arts and Crafts detailing in the main house, it was simplified to create a clean, contemporary look in the in-law. The three-point arch, also a favorite of ancient Roman builders, offers a graceful transition between rooms.

ABOVE: Although the kitchen seems simple at first glance, it contains a full complement of appliances and a number of sophisticated details. The rich green paint, which would be overwhelming on a larger wall, imparts personality as an accent color. And the porcelain tile niche above the range is a focal point with a classic air.

Thanks to high ceilings and a generous number of windows on three sides, all the rooms feel bright and airy any time of day. But when the morning sun streams in, the living room and the breakfast nook are the places to be.

The nook looks out onto the patio and into a beautifully composed kitchen. There's a full battery of appliances in the kitchen, including a full-width stove, yet the view from the nook is symmetrical and serene. A handsome polished steel range and matching hood are flanked by light-hued maple cabinets and banded by a white porcelain tile backsplash with a recessed niche. The bathroom features comparable details.

The patio gets a lot of use in warm weather, too, and once the screen of flowering vines is grown in, you'll hardly know the cars are there. It will feel more park than parking.

CENTER: A narrow window in the corner gives your eyes a place to wander when you're working at the sink, and illuminates objects in the open shelves. The playful layout of two tiny sinks set at an angle emerged out of necessity: with so many appliances in close quarters there simply wasn't room for a single larger sink.

LEFT: The understated charm of the apartment continues in the bathroom. Look closely and you'll see a reflection of the arch that defines the shower-tub enclosure.

THINKING INSIDE THE ENVELOPE

Enlarging the footprint of a house may require conforming to a spate of zoning regulations and codes that can greatly impact the schedule and cost of a project. Do everything possible to avoid this by maximizing space within the envelope and getting rid of space-wasting features you don't need. In the Tramutola conversion, for example, space was gained for a generous closet by removing the foundation for a brick fireplace upstairs—after first decommissioning the fireplace. They were also able to add many tall windows without altering the unit's energy profile. Those windows and the high ceilings, in turn, allowed light to reach far into the unit—essential for making a small space feel bigger. □

KEEPING THE TRIM SIMPLE IS A SMART MOVE if you're thinking about renting the in-law at some point. Simply shaped molding costs less to install and is less likely to conflict with whatever furniture style your tenant brings in. Here, however, using simple trim was an explicit design choice, not just economizing.

CHAPTER 3

choosing appliances, fixtures, and materials

THE PRODUCTS HIGHLIGHTED in this chapter are well suited to life in an in-law unit: most of the appliances are compact, easy to use, and energy-efficient; the surface materials are durable and easy to maintain. But this survey is just a first step of the research you'll want to do. Let's start with some specific product features to look for—and a few to avoid. The Appendix (p. 212) lists manufacturer websites where you can learn more.

Before we dig in, one piece of advice: buy quality. The long-term cost of operating any appliance will dwarf its purchase price. Better appliances, especially compact

units, will last longer, have more advanced features, and run more efficiently.

KITCHEN APPLIANCES

Kitchens consume more energy than any other room in the house—nearly 30 percent of the utility bill—and refrigerators and freezers together gobble almost two-thirds of the kitchen's total. (Ovens and cooktops account for about 25 percent and dishwashers 10 percent.) These figures should interest anyone thinking of adding an in-law unit, especially if you plan to share a utility meter with your tenant and have to guesstimate his or her share.

REFRIGERATOR/FREEZERS

One of the first appliances to go compact, fridges are available in varying sizes; the smallest models are only 18 in. wide and short enough to fit easily under counters.

Look for: Freezers on top or bottom (side-by-side doors waste energy), manual defrost option (auto-defrost is convenient, but inefficient), variable-speed compressors (they save energy by running at lower speeds during low-use periods), or vacuum-panel insulation (more energy conserving than foam insulation). Consider ¾-size fridges, too, whose capacities and energy use are a compromise between compact and full-size models.

Smart but pricey: Refrigerator drawers (especially helpful for folks with mobility issues) and custom-cooling sensors that create different temperature zones so veggies don't wilt.

Avoid: Thru-door ice and water dispensers (energy-guzzlers); 15-in.-wide models are only about 12 in. wide inside and are too narrow to hold much.

OVENS

When it comes to conventional ovens, electric ovens are two or three times more energy-efficient than gas models. Because

IS YOUR ELECTRICAL SYSTEM ADEQUATELY SIZED?

The only sure way to know if there's enough capacity to add an in-law unit is to calculate the electrical loads to be added. A licensed electrician can do this or, for diehard DIYers, there are plenty of wiring books that walk you through load calculations. Here's a rule of thumb. If you have a 150-amp or a 200-amp breaker panel and there are unused breaker slots in it, you probably have enough capacity, unless you plan to add an electric range, electric heating, or other big energy users. If you have a 100-amp panel, which is considered minimal these days, the answer is less clear. In any event, have a licensed electrician assess your system and do all upgrades.

DON'T PLACE A REFRIGERATOR OR FREEZER next to a heat source or an appliance with heating elements such as an oven or dishwasher. It will heat the outside of the refrigerator, requiring its compressor to run more often to dissipate that heat, which will needlessly run up your energy bill.

ovens don't require the fast heat-up of cooktops, electric ovens are comparable to gas stoves in most respects, including cooking times and evenness of heating. Gas appliances must also be vented to be safe. (Gas appliances are popular, in part, because natural gas or propane is cheaper than electricity in many areas.)

Microwave ovens are by far the most energy-efficient cooking appliance, and their compact size makes them ideal for in-laws. Shop around and you can save a bundle: prices vary wildly for models with essentially the same features. Only a few companies actually make microwave ovens, so don't pay more for a fancier label if a lesser model has the features you want.

Look for: OTC- (over the counter) and OTR- (over the range) mounted microwave models free up counter space and OTR models double as range hoods to exhaust cooking smells. To better exhaust full-size stoves, some OTR models have hoods with slide-out vents.

Smart but pricey: If you're a serious cook, consider convection microwaves that allow you to roast, bake, broil, or brown food.

Avoid: Expensive models if you'll only use the device to heat soup or make popcorn.

COOKTOPS

Separate cooktops are popular because they aren't attached to a stove, so there's more design flexibility when fitting them into a small kitchen. Many cooks prefer a gas cooktop because it heats up quickly and can be controlled precisely. But would-be landlords might want to think thrice about the open flames, combustion gases, and wasteful energy use of gas cooktops. Instead, consider:

Induction cooktops transfer electrical energy directly (magnetically) to special ferrous cookware, making this technology 80% to 85% efficient. Induction cooktops are safer because the cooking surface itself does not heat up. Drawbacks: Induction cooktops are very expensive, and you can use only certain types of cookware with them.

Radiant ceramic cooktops have radiant heating elements under a ceramic glass top, so they heat quickly and are simple to clean. These cooktops are about 75% efficient, which is comparable to electric coils but radiant models heat faster. Price: intermediate to high.

Electric coil cooktops, the oldest technology, are on the low end of the cost/glamour continuum, so they are used mostly in budget appliances. Drawbacks: Slow to heat and tedious to clean if a pot boils over onto the coils.

Hybrid microwave/convection ovens such as the GE Advantium® give small kitchens a lot of firepower. The 30-in.-wide oven fits easily below an upper cabinet and offers three cooking modes, including one that browns and broils like a conventional oven. The oven's integral range hood also vents the two-burner cooktop below.

RANGE HOODS

Range hoods are required by code because they remove excess moisture and cooking smells. Ideally, a range hood should be directly over and slightly wider than the stove or cooktop. If your house adjoins the in-law unit, your tenant's range hood will contribute to your health and comfort, too.

Look for: A 100 cfm (cu. ft./min.) wall-mounted hood with a variable-speed fan should adequately vent a four-burner, 30-in.-wide range. More is not necessarily better when sizing range hoods because bigger exhaust fans are noisy. A midsize hood averages 3 sones (a noise rating); a refrigerator registers 1 sone.

Avoid: Downdraft or side-draft vents that pop up from a counter area to suck away fumes—they also suck away cooking heat. Especially avoid recirculating range hood fans, which remove only odors, not combustion gases or moisture.

DISHWASHERS

In the last decade, dishwashers have changed from scullery maids to Cinderellas. Pushed by consumer demands and ENERGY STAR® standards, they offer a dazzling array of features and are as careful about conserving water as energy, with normal washing cycles using less than 6 gal. Look for energy-factor (EF) ratings of at least 0.65, the ENERGY STAR minimum.

Compact models: Slender, 18-in.-wide dishwashers tuck into tight spots yet still hold eight place settings. Under-the-sink models fit nicely beneath a 6-in.-deep kitchen sink, space that's often underused. Dishwasher drawers typically have about half the capacity of a full-size dishwasher,

but drawers can't be beat for accessibility, especially for users with bad backs or mobility issues. They're also a smart choice for single tenants who run small loads.

Look for: Quieter models are well insulated, with separate motors for washing and draining; go for dB noise-ratings of 40 to 50 or less (lower is better). Also desirable: steam-cleaning cycles (more efficient and gentler on wineglasses and fine china), half-load wash options, adjustable storage racks, and soil sensors (they determine if dishes are clean enough or if the wash cycle should continue).

Smart but pricey: Condensation drying, which saves energy by varying rinse-water temperatures and using a small fan to help remove moisture.

Avoid: Dishwashers without a no-heat drying option. Use pot-and-pans-washing and heated-drying cycles as little as possible (they're energy slurpers).

COMPACT KITCHEN MODULES

Compact kitchen modules, also called kitchenettes, combine several functions in a single freestanding appliance. If a module contains gas burners or a gas oven, it must also be vented outdoors; the great majority of all-in-one units are all-electric, however.

As you might expect, features and prices of kitchenettes vary widely, as do the quality of their housings. A basic, white enamel steel 30-in.-wide base unit, with a 3.8 cu. ft. refrigerator, a 2-burner cooktop, and a lightweight sink costs about $600. In comparison, a 72-in.-wide console of upper and lower cabinets in custom colors, a 6-cu.-ft. refrigerator with auto-defrost, 4 electric burners, a built-

BEFORE ORDERING A COMPACT KITCHEN MODULE, look for customer-service feedback about the product you're considering. Kitchen modules are bulky and expensive to ship long distances; choosing a supplier with a local warehouse may help lower costs.

in 24-in. electric range with a porcelain enamel finish and a range hood, a heavy stainless steel sink, a microwave oven, and roughly 20 cu. ft. of cabinet storage will run about $4,000—a typical mid-range price. And you can customize a compact kitchen by assembling stylish components from giants such as IKEA®, who will walk you through the planning process.

KITCHEN CABINET SPACE-MISERS

Each in-law unit is unique. One advantage of choosing individual cabinet components is that you can combine specialty drawers, inserts, and hardware to maximize storage, even the tricky spaces under a sink, in the back of shelves, and in cabinet corners (see the photos on the facing page).

One of the great advances in making storage more accessible is storage shelving mounted on drawer glides so it can be pulled out. Items in the back of fixed shelves are invariably blocked by the stuff in front. This might be acceptable for storing "the good china" that you use infrequently, but it's a waste for a tenant with one set of dishes and little room to store pots, pans, dishes, and groceries. Specifying drawers instead of base-cabinet shelves is an especially good way to gain access to items in the back without a lot of straining, lifting, or rearranging, making this a great option for elders and those with limited strength or range of motion.

Look for: Side-mounted, ball-bearing drawer slides rated for 75-lb. or 100-lb. loads (a drawer full of cast-iron gets heavy); three-quarter or full-extension slides will enable you to reach items at the back; soft-close mechanisms (to prevent drawers or doors slamming and damaging stored items; they're quiet, too).

Smart but pricey: The more complex the hardware—some corner-cabinet pullout mechanisms slide *and* pivot—the more it'll cost.

ABOVE TOP: YesterTec's® Stealth Kitchen Module houses 120V appliances, including a hybrid microwave/oven and exhaust hood, a two-burner ceramic cooktop, an undercounter refrigerator/freezer, a dishwasher drawer, a sink, and a fair amount of storage. For safety, the cooktop and oven won't operate when the doors are closed. Available in many furniture styles, kitchen consoles are one way to make multifunctional rooms look good, too.

ABOVE: The kitchen module closed.

As the front baskets of these Häfele® units pull out and swivel 90°, the back baskets move into the cabinet opening, where they can be pulled forward. This improves access to stored items in blind corner cabinets.

BELOW: Pots, pans, and lids stored on shelves invariably get mixed, making it hard to find the item you need. Rev-a-shelf's® two-tiered cookware organizer holds up to seven lids and is sturdy enough to support cast-iron cookware.

LEFT: Pullout pantries enable you to store things in deep, narrow spaces that might otherwise go unused. Make sure the pullout's slides can bear the weight because fully loaded shelves are heavy.

ROOM TO WORK

When planning an in-law kitchen (or any other), it's useful to note the standard heights for cabinets and shelves because these dimensions are optimal for the largest number of adult users. It's also essential to provide enough counter workspace and enough room between cabinets and appliances so users can open doors and drawers or, if need be, walk by. Pass-through space is especially important in galley kitchens.

Recommended Counter Space and Clearances

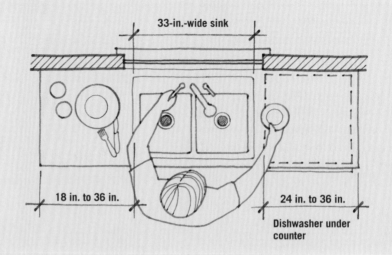

33-in.-wide sink

18 in. to 36 in.

24 in. to 36 in.

Dishwasher under counter

Standard Cabinet Dimensions

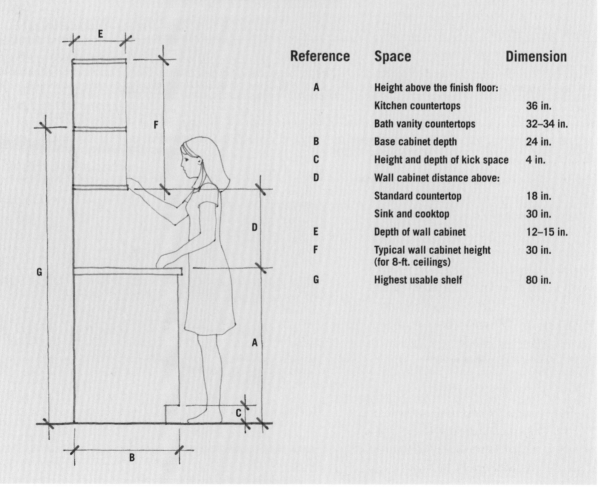

Reference	Space	Dimension
A	**Height above the finish floor:**	
	Kitchen countertops	36 in.
	Bath vanity countertops	32–34 in.
B	Base cabinet depth	24 in.
C	Height and depth of kick space	4 in.
D	Wall cabinet distance above:	
	Standard countertop	18 in.
	Sink and cooktop	30 in.
E	Depth of wall cabinet	12–15 in.
F	Typical wall cabinet height (for 8-ft. ceilings)	30 in.
G	Highest usable shelf	80 in.

WATER HEATERS

If your in-law unit is detached or its kitchen and bathroom are distant from the house, it may be most cost-effective to install a tankless water heater instead of a standard tank-type unit. Although it's more expensive to install than a conventional water heater and its efficiency ratings are roughly the same, a tankless unit costs far less to operate. With no tank, it won't waste energy keeping a tankful of water hot in readiness for someone showering or washing dishes. A tankless water heater produces hot water on-demand, and as much as you want. Typically hung on the inside surface of an exterior wall, it can also be installed on the outside surface in mild climates. In any case, the units are far more compact than conventional water heaters, a boon for small spaces.

Look for: A 140,000-BTU-input tankless unit should do for one or two users if its EF (energy factor) is 0.82 or greater. Gas-fired models are more efficient but must be vented, so there are fewer indoor installation options. You may also have to run a larger gas line to supply the unit. An electric tankless unit of similar capacity will probably require a 240-volt/60-amp breaker. Have a licensed plumber size and install your tankless unit; they are more complicated than conventional water heaters.

A caveat: If your in-law unit shares a wet wall with the house, plumbing is already close by. It may be more cost-effective to tap into existing pipes if the current water heater has enough capacity. Here again, though, consult a plumber who has worked with similar installations before.

BATHROOM FIXTURES

A properly planned bathroom is a joy to use. But some bathroom fixtures cost more than your first car and sport more bling than a Vegas chorus line. So we'll limit our inquiry

LIGHTING DESIGN

Having enough light in an in-law unit is important, particularly if the occupant is older. General lighting can come from recessed ceiling cans, surface-mounted fixtures, track lighting, and cove uplighting. Provide 2w (watts) of incandescent or 1w of fluorescent light per sq. ft. of kitchen area. Even illumination is the goal of general lighting, whereas task lighting should be concentrated over work areas such as sinks, countertops, and islands. Here, recessed cans, pendants, and undercabinet fixtures (T5 or halogen strips) are the best choices.

Tankless water heaters are especially well suited to in-law suites with space constraints or to suites whose kitchens and bathrooms are too far from an existing water heater in the main house.

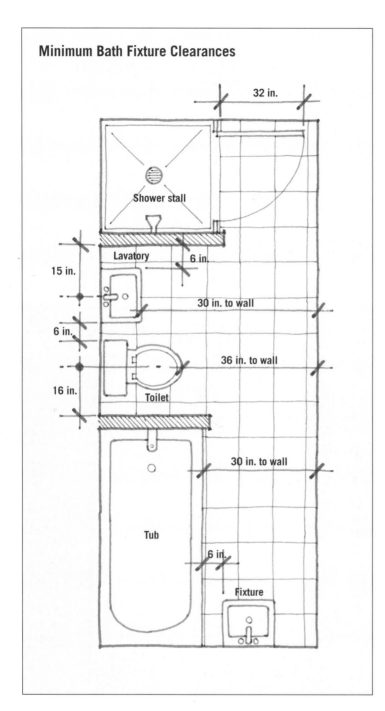

Minimum Bath Fixture Clearances

32 in.

Shower stall

Lavatory

15 in.

6 in.

6 in.

30 in. to wall

Toilet

36 in. to wall

16 in.

Tub

30 in. to wall

6 in.

Fixture

to fixtures and accessories with a practical bent. These are the ones that conserve water, energy, and space; are affordable and easy to maintain; and will help to protect the user from falls, scalds, and other mishaps.

TUBS

As a lifelong soaker, I love tubs, but I wouldn't put a standard tub into an in-law unit if I could avoid it. They guzzle water and energy and hog space, and their weight when filled requires beefed-up framing to support them unless they sit on a slab. And the gymnastics of using a hot-water-filled vessel slick with soapy residue make them iffy, safety-wise. Granted, you can't read a newspaper in the shower but showers trump tubs in most other respects.

Look for: Compact walk-in tubs are well suited to the tight spaces of an in-law unit housing an elderly or disabled person. But their high cost ($2,000 to $8,000 is typical) is unwarranted for anyone but a special-needs user. Most are contoured, with slip-resistant benches and front- or side-opening doors that seal tightly to contain bathwater. Most feature a lever-type closing device.

Smart but pricey: Homeowners who can afford a walk-in tub in the first place may want to spend a bit more for accessories such as anti-scald mixing valves, extra massage jets, and power lifts that raise and lower users.

SHOWER SURROUNDS

Surrounds—the finish surfaces enclosing a shower or shower/tub combination—take many forms, from an economical single-piece module to a custom tile job costing thousands of dollars. There is tremendous variation in composition, ease of installation, durability, aesthetics, and, of course, expense.

Look for: Single-piece shower modules molded from fiberglass or acrylic are the

Designed for individuals with mobility problems, Safety Tubs'® walk-in tubs are easier to access, ideal for the tight spaces of in-law units, and more water conserving than standard 5-ft. tubs.

BELOW: Architect Cheryl Mohr maximized usable space in this 5½-ft. by 9-ft. bathroom by replacing a tub with low-curb shower—in effect, creating a wet room. A floor-to-ceiling mirror at one end doubles the space visually.

most popular and economical surrounds. Modules are also available as multipiece units well suited to renovations, when it might not be possible to maneuver a one-piece module through existing doorways. The knock against modules is that they look and feel like plastic and sound flimsy if you bump them. So if your in-law unit shares a wet wall with the house, you may want to insulate the backside of the unit to muffle the sound or buy a more expensive unit, which will have thicker walls. But the fact remains, modules are, when properly installed, durable, easy to maintain, and, above all, waterproof. A landlord's dream.

Smart but pricey: Custom tilework is the best way to maximize usable space in a small bathroom with a shower. For years, Europeans have enlarged their shower spaces by doing away with shower walls, curbs, and thresholds within a bathroom. The result is an open, completely tiled *wet room* whose floors slope to a central drain. This open layout is accessible to all users. As long as the lavatory and toilet are at least 1 ft. away from the general shower spray pattern, few drops will land on them, and if they do, no big deal. If fixtures are closer or if open spaces don't agree with you, however, it's easy enough to add a curb to corral the water, a glass wall to contain splashes, or a shower curtain.

SHOWER HARDWARE

Shower hardware usually comes packaged as three matched components: a showerhead, a tub spout, and a control lever that operates a mixing valve behind the wall. Showerheads conserve water in two ways, by constricting flow and directing flow.

Look for: Well-engineered, reduced-flow showerheads needn't feel like a meager drizzle; they can increase pressure by varying apertures. Makes such as Oxygenic® use less than 1.3 gal. per min. (gpm), yet deliver a robust spray. Directing the flow is a fancy way of saying that if you can aim the water at the spot you're washing, you'll use less water. Thus installing a handheld showerhead—preferably one that can also be fixed to the wall—is a great addition to any in-law unit's bathroom. Handhelds are relatively inexpensive, versatile, and a breeze to install. You can wash your old mum's hair or rinse the garden out of the dog with equal ease. And using a handheld, disabled people can remain seated while showering.

Smart but pricey: Many high-end products direct water flow to specific areas, whether as rotating showerheads mounted on a pivoting arm, a separate pulsating handheld combined with a large fixed head (PULSE Showerspas Molokai), or a vertical shower panel with multiple heads designed to replace a standard fixed showerhead in 15 minutes (Hansgrohe® BodyShower).

LAVATORIES

It doesn't take much room to wash your hands and so, no surprise, there are many little lavs (bathroom sinks) to choose from, some of them barely large enough to fit a man's hands. Kohler®'s smallest round lavatory has a 10⅝-in. inner diameter, and the Porcher® Elfe, a rectangular lav, has a

The GROHE® Freehander® provides two overhead sprays or, when pivoted down, two jets for body washing—ideal for a seated shower. Sprays can also be adjusted to normal, pulse, or water-saving modes.

basin that measures 12¾ in. by 6⅝ in. So finding *small* won't be a problem.

Look for: Lavatories should be easy to clean, stain-resistant, and tough enough to withstand daily use. Enameled cast iron is the workhorse of lavs. Vitreous china is the most popular, a bit delicate, yet also easy to clean. Wall-hung sinks, having no legs or cabinet beneath, are the easiest to clean under—a legitimate concern when housing an elderly parent—and the easiest for a person in a wheelchair to get close to (see the photo below). Of the types mounted to countertops or vanities, undercounter sinks are the easiest to keep clean because there's no lip in which crud can collect. Regarding hardware, a single-lever faucet is simplest and most compatible with the single-hole design of most small sinks—and the easiest to use by most people.

With just enough room for your toes under this corner lav, you won't dally while shaving or putting on makeup. But it successfully transforms a former closet into a half-bath.

There are even offset faucets (see p. 187) that really scrimp on space, but they cost more.

Avoid: Lavs made of porous materials such as slate, soapstone, or unglazed ceramics can stain. Hand-painted sinks are lovely but become tiresome if the decor changes or you chip them.

TOILETS AND WASHLETS

Fresh water resources are under such enormous strains that water riots happen around the world. Much to their credit, toilet manufacturers have dramatically improved the efficiency of their products.

Look for: Dual-flush toilets allow users to choose a lower-volume flush for liquid wastes. Where toilets once required 3.5 gal. per flush, TOTO's® Aqua® dual-flush (right) model flushes solid wastes with 1.6 gal. and liquid wastes with 0.9 gal. This can save 1,000 to 1,500 gal. per person annually. Of the three principal types of toilets (see the drawing on p. 62), low-profile models are typically the easier to clean because there's no seam between the tank and the seat. Low-profile units are the quietest type as well, making them a good choice for bathrooms that adjoin bedrooms or share a wet wall with a house.

Smart but pricey: Wall-hung toilets tend to be the most expensive to buy and install but are unrivaled in maximizing space in small bathrooms—because their tanks are hidden in the wall behind the toilet seat. Hanging the toilet greatly simplifies mopping the floor, too. When you can't achieve minimum clearances (see p. 58) between the toilet and other fixtures, a corner toilet may save the day; its beveled tank fits nicely into that oddest of spaces.

Special mention: Among many laudable water-conserving products, TOTO's Washlet® personal cleansing system is a standout. The Washlet is a

Dual-flush toilets such as the Toto Aqua (top) use two separate flush modes (bottom) to save more water than standard 1.6-gal. flush toilets, making them worth the extra cost in areas where water restrictions are severe.

Toilet Types and Sizes

Two-Piece Toilet
The taller tank height generates more flushing force

One-Piece Toilet
Characterized by a streamlined, low-profile design that simplifies cleaning

Wall-Hung Toilet
Good for small bathrooms because the tank is in the wall

Bowl Shapes
Round bowls are shorter but wider than oval bowls

26¾ in.

30⅝ in.

toilet seat with a few well-designed accessories that spray warm, aerated water on those parts that need frequent attention and then gently dry the works with warm air. In other words, it's a hands-free, high-tech bidet without the expense and bother of adding another fixture to a bathroom. At the heart of the system are a retractable, self-cleaning nozzle and a wireless remote control that allows users to adjust water temperature and other variables. It's ideal for elderly people, someone who's just had an operation or given birth, and anyone unable to tend to matters themselves.

BATHROOM FANS

Bathroom fans have become increasingly powerful, quiet, and replete with extra features such as heaters, lights, humidity sensors, and so on. As a rule, size the fan 1 cfm (cubic feet per minute) for each sq. ft. of floor space, up to 100 sq. ft. For baths larger than 100 sq. ft., add 50 cfm for each fixture (toilet, lav, and shower) and 100 cfm for a hot tub.

Look for: A decade ago, bath fans averaged a 3-sone rating; today's models are closer to 1.5 sones, which is comparable to the noise a refrigerator makes. And mid- to high-end models are quieter yet, with some achieving 0.3 or 0.4 sone ratings. The sizes of the fan and the ducts will also affect the noise level. Fans should stay on for a while after you leave the shower or use the toilet. More expensive models have an integral timer switch, a humidity sensor, or some combination of both. If there's a fan/light combo, the fan should continue running after the light is off.

Smart but pricey: Most bath fans seem so noisy because they're located right over your head. If you want a quieter solution, put the intake grille in the usual place, but install an inline fan farther away—say, in an attic or a crawlspace.

LAUNDRY APPLIANCES

Today's washers and dryers give home-owners real choices when it comes to saving water and energy, so compare ENERGY STAR MEF (modified energy factor) ratings: the higher the MEF rating, the more efficient the appliance. Washers also have WF (water factor) ratings: the lower the number, the more water it conserves. Although washers and dryers are dis-cussed separately below, they should be purchased at the same time as matched sets based on their capacity and other factors. (If you choose a washer-dryer combination, both functions are housed in one machine.)

If your in-law unit is attached or close to the house and you already have energy-efficient full-size laundry appliances, it might make sense to share them with your tenant. Ideally, the laundry should be located in a common area such as an unfinished basement or a garage, which each party can access and use without disturbing the other. Compact machines are not much smaller than full-size ones and often cost just as much.

WASHING MACHINES

Most of the energy consumed in washing clothes comes from heating water, so the most energy-efficient machines also tend to use less water. ENERGY STAR–rated washers must have a minimum 1.72 MEF and a maximum 8.0 WF.

Look for: Front-loading models (also called horizontal-axis washers) generally cost more than top loaders, but front loaders get clothes cleaner, are quieter, spin clothes drier and damage them less, and consume less energy, water, and detergent. Hence, they're cheaper to operate long-term. If space-conservation is an issue, consider stackables; better-

quality stackables usually include a front-loading washer.

Smart but pricey: A steam feature is relatively new but coming on strong because it's better at removing stains and removing wrinkles and consumes less water. Vibration reduction technology (VRT) has migrated from commercial to residential machines; look for customer reviews of washers with VRT because most VRT spec sheets are unintelligible. (Putting vibration-dampening pads under

Stackable washer and dryer setups are space conserving if you have the room to go up. Buying matched machines is essential with stackables to ensure balanced, vibration-free operation.

each foot of the machine may do the same thing at less expense.)

Avoid: Roll-out compact models. Compacts cost about the same as stationary top-loaders and don't really save much space: full-size washers are 27 in. wide; compacts are 24 in. Plus, when not in use, a rollout is taking up space somewhere. Lastly, because such models are not stationary, they vibrate more and make more noise.

CLOTHES DRYERS

The first consideration for a dryer is whether it's electric or gas, which is primarily a decision based on which service is already in place. Most dryers require a 4-in.-diameter duct to the outside to vent moisture.

Look for: ENERGY STAR–rated machines whether compact or full-size models. Both types have roughly the same size housing (24 in. wide vs. 29 in. wide) but the smaller loads of compact models (3.5 cu. ft. to 5.0 cu. ft.) make them cheaper to operate for one or two people. The capacity of full-size models (up to 7.5 cu. ft.) is better suited to a family.

Smart but pricey: Condensation dryers cost more but eliminate the need to vent moisture: Water condenses and exits through a small drain, which gives you more flexibility in locating the laundry. Lint-filter warning lights are worthwhile because excessive lint buildup slows drying, wastes energy, and can catch fire. A steaming feature seems counterintuitive but clothes come out less wrinkled.

WASHER-DRYER COMBOS

A washer-dryer combo is a single unit that washes and dries. Combos can be quite expensive ($800 to $1,600) and take some getting used to, but they deliver in all respects: saving energy, water, and, notably, space. Unlike most separate compact units, combos can fit comfortably under a kitchen counter. They run on 120 volts. Because the drying cycle of the machine uses condensation drying, there's no need to vent moisture via a duct. What takes getting used to is the operation time: from putting clothes in dirty to taking them out clean and dry takes 3 to 4 hours on the normal setting.

COUNTERTOP AND FLOORING MATERIALS

Though subject to different uses, both countertops and floors get a lot of wear and abuse and both frequently come in contact with water. Thus, whether choosing countertop or flooring materials for an in-law unit, homeowners consistently put durability, ease of maintenance, and reasonable cost at the top of their lists. In addition to those traits, the charts on the facing page include other use-specific ratings to help you make your choice.

SMOKE ALARMS AND SPRINKLERS

When you meet with the city planning department, a planner will describe the fire safety elements that will be required for your in-law unit, including the location and type of smoke alarms. Though the practices and devices described in this section are widely accepted, your local fire codes have the final say.

SMOKE ALARMS

Smoke alarms are required by code in sleeping areas (or just outside them) and on every level of a house, including the basement, whether it's finished or not. Battery-powered alarms are usually acceptable in existing residences, but in new construction or substantial remodels, codes may call for hardwired alarms with battery backup. Hardwired alarms must be interlinked so that if one sounds, all do.

COUNTERTOP CHOICES

CHARACTERISTIC	PLASTIC LAMINATE	SOLID SURFACE	QUARTZ COMPOSITE	CERAMIC TILE	STONE	CONCRETE	WOOD
DURABILITY, SCRATCH RESISTANCE	Fair	Excellent*	Excellent	Good	Good†	Good	Fair‡
EASE OF CLEANING	Excellent	Excellent	Excellent	Fair §	Excellent	Good	Fair
STAIN RESISTANCE	Good	Good	Excellent	Fair	Fair	Poor	Poor
WATER RESISTANCE	Good	Excellent	Excellent	Fair	Good	Good	Poor
HEAT RESISTANCE	Poor	Fair	Good	Excellent	Good	Excellent	Poor
COST	$	$$$	$$–$$$	$$	$$$	$–$$	$$

*Material scratches, but scratches are easily sanded out.

‡ Durability depends on type of wood and finish; wood is generally a bad choice near sinks and water.

† Harder stones (granite) wear well; softer stones (soapstone) scratch and stain easily.

§ Glazed tiles resist stains, water, and heat; but grout joints deteriorate if not sealed and maintained.

FLOORING CHOICES

CHARACTERISTIC	SOLID WOOD	ENGINEERED WOOD	LAMINATE	RESILIENT FLOORING	BAMBOO	PALM	CORK	TILE & STONE	CONCRETE
DURABILITY	Good	Very good	Excellent	Excellent	Very good	Very good	Good*	Excellent	Excellent
REQUIRED MAINTENANCE	Sweep regularly	Sweep regularly	Damp mop	Damp mop	Sweep regularly	Sweep regularly	Sweep or damp mop	Wet mop	Wet mop
WATER RESISTANCE†	Poor	Fair	Good	Good to excellent	Poor to fair	Poor to fair	Poor	Excellent	Excellent
COMFORT UNDERFOOT	Flexes	Flexes	Flexes	Soft	Flexes	Flexes	Soft	Hard	Hard
GREEN CREDS	Yes	Mixed	No	Lino, yes vinyl, no‡	Yes	Yes	Yes	Yes	Mixed
COST§	$–$$$	$–$$	$	$	$–$$	$$	$$–$$$	$$–$$$	$–$$

*Durable, but deforms if furniture sits on same spot for too long.

‡ Linoleum and recycled rubber are considered green, vinyl is not.

† Correct persistent moisture problems before converting any area to living space.

§ Costs do not reflect installation charges.

Types. There are several types of smoke alarms used in residences. The most commonly used ones are *ionization* types, which use a tiny amount of a radioactive isotope to detect airborne ions associated with freely burning fires. *Photoelectric* or optical alarms shoot a beam of light to detect the presence of larger smoke particles and thus are better at detecting smoldering fires that have not yet burst into flame. *Heat-sensing* alarms sound when temperatures reach a certain threshold. Because steam or cooking fumes can sometimes trigger the first two types, heat-sensing types are the least likely to give false or nuisance alarms. But each type has its strengths, so several types are sometimes employed in one residence.

Location of alarms. Smoke alarms can be installed on a ceiling or high on a wall, but ceilings are the best location. On a flat ceiling, a ceiling-mounted alarm must be at least 4 in. away from an adjacent wall; on a vaulted ceiling, the alarm must be at least 4 in. below the peak and within 3 ft. horizontally. Whether ceiling- or wall-mounted, a smoke alarm must not be located within the 4-in.-wide dead-air space: smoke does not circulate into corners.

FIRE SPRINKLER SYSTEMS

In the event of a fire, residential fire sprinkler systems give people inside a little more time to escape safely and firefighters more opportunity to enter and suppress the fire before it burns the house to the ground. Local codes may require sprinkler systems in all new homes; many locales require them in all new accessory dwelling units. Where sprinklers are required, they are generally installed in living areas only, not in garages, attics, or storage spaces.

Sprinkler systems connect to a system of pressurized water pipes and are configured in two ways. A *multipurpose system*, tied to the house's water-supply system, generally costs less because it uses the same cold-water pipes that feed fixtures throughout the house. A *stand-alone system*, on the other hand, is separate from the house's supply system. Sprinkler heads vary, but standard coverage per head is an area 12 ft. by 12 ft. in size and some heads are rated to cover up to 20 ft. by 20 ft. □

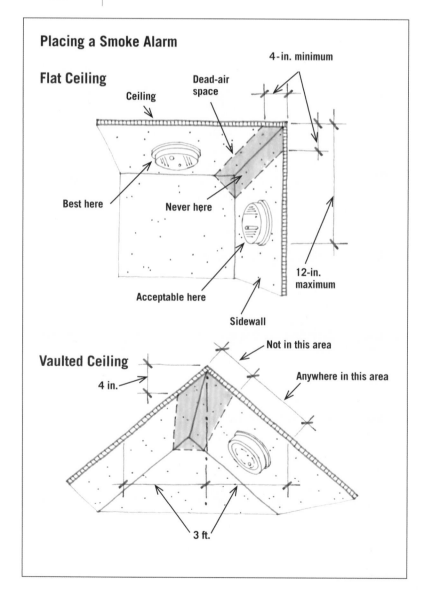

WIRELESSLY LINKED SMOKE ALARMS CAN SIMPLIFY FIRE-SAFETY COMPLIANCE, especially if you are remodeling part of your house or adding on to create an in-law unit. Ask your building department if wireless links are approved for your area.

Placing a Smoke Alarm

Flat Ceiling

Ceiling

Dead-air space

4-in. minimum

Best here

Never here

Acceptable here

Sidewall

12-in. maximum

Vaulted Ceiling

Not in this area

Anywhere in this area

4 in.

3 ft.

TO HELP FIREFIGHTERS FIND YOUR IN-LAW UNIT, most city codes require that the unit's address be clearly visible from the street. Or, if the unit is behind the house, the unit's address must be affixed to the house or to a separate post in the yard, facing the street.

DISAPPEARING BEDS

In 1900, William Murphy invented his first folding bed because the standard bed in his one-bedroom San Francisco apartment took up most of the floor space, leaving no room to entertain. Thanks to their ingenuity, Murphy beds were an immediate hit and the silent-movie gag of malfunctioning Murphys swallowing up sleepers only added to their fame. Today, dozens of companies make beds that fold into wall alcoves, hide in custom cabinets, and disappear into ceilings. Kits are even available that allow you to make your own. See Resources on p. 214 for more information.

Disappearing beds save valuable space and come in a variety of styles and sizes. This one can be built from plans to hold a full- or queen-size mattress. It converts to a desk (photo above) during the day.

grandma's home

Family has always mattered to Julie. When her kids were small, she and her husband moved into the house that she grew up in so she could care for her ailing father. Perhaps it was only natural, then, that some years later Julie invited her daughter Denise and her kids to move into the family home after Julie's husband passed away. Grandkids are a great antidote for houses that have become too big and too quiet.

When its steel siding fully oxidizes, the in-law's exterior will have the same colors as the stucco and brick main house. The area at the front door has a sloping concrete apron to shed water rather than a raised threshold, which could limit access.

Floor Plan

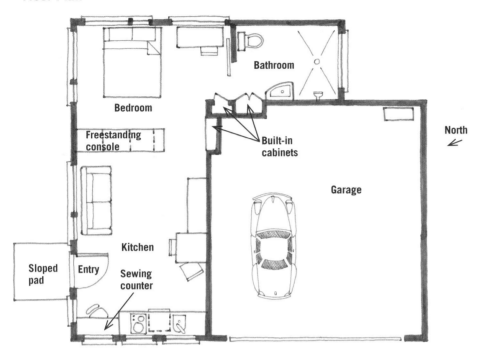

Bedroom

Bathroom

Freestanding console

Built-in cabinets

Garage

North

Kitchen

Sloped pad

Entry

Sewing counter

Living under one roof wasn't what she had in mind, however. To give her daughter privacy and herself a break from climbing stairs, Julie decided to build a single-story in-law for herself in the backyard. Curious about green building, she began attending seminars and asking friends if they knew of any green-minded architects, which eventually led her to Fred Hyer and his associate, Patricia Fontana-Narell. Hyer's portfolio had a large dose of modern houses with oddball details such as car windshields recycled as door awnings, which delighted Julie.

However, Julie had already figured out the best place for the in-law unit: in the corner of the lot, right up against the garage. But exactly how it would fit was a stumper. The garage was so close to the east property line that even the tiny footprint allowed by the city—450 sq. ft.—couldn't be built as a rectangle without encroaching on setback lines in the back, or in the front, impeding access to the backyard. In the end, Julie settled on an L-shaped floor plan that wrapped around the garage.

ACCESSIBLE LIVING

That decided, the design evolved smoothly. The front door was logically situated on the corner closest to the house, facing the backyard, to provide privacy, pleasant views, and the shortest walk for Julie. Just inside the door are public spaces to welcome and entertain guests—the living, dining, and kitchen areas. Of the three, kitchens most need natural light, so a fire engine red galley kitchen runs along the west wall. In this unit, most of the good light comes

MAKE TIME FOR DESIGN. If you are fortunate enough to find an architect who listens, return the favor. Give design professionals enough time to do their jobs, then ponder each design they present— even if you think you already know what you want. Discarded designs often contain great details.

REALITY-CHECK FLOOR PLANS.

When refining floor plans for an in-law, measure the largest items you own to make sure there will be room for them. Measuring furniture, large plates and platters, and the dimensions of your current closets can also help you decide what you need to get rid of.

Julie, Denise, and a 1940 Chevy® Coupe in front of the garage.

Over the front door, a back hatch window from a Porsche® 928 was reincarnated as an awning.

from the west, with some indirect light from the north. The garage blocks southern light; eastern light in the morning enters through the bedroom.

Because the in-law was limited to 450 sq. ft. by city codes, the architects had to hustle to get enough closet space. One set of cabinets was cantilevered into the garage space. The garage had room to spare and, as important, the gained space wasn't considered part of the 450 sq. ft.

By default, the bedroom and bath are in the back, far from the big house and the traffic noise of the street. Because the back leg of the L was too small for a bedroom, that's where the bathroom landed, farthest from the public

ABOVE: No shrinking violet, Julie chose fire engine red cabinets for her compact kitchen. The cabinets are custom-made of FSC-certified plywood; the countertops are concrete and were cast off-site.

LEFT: The bathroom features salvaged beams, a sliding door with barn hardware, and a shower large enough for someone in a wheelchair—or two grandchildren muddy from playing in the garden. One end of the custom concrete sink tapers so it's easier to roll by, whereas the ample shoulder at the other end is a helpful place for a wheelchair user to place soap or shampoo while showering. Note: no threshold between rooms.

DESIGN FOR THE FUTURE. You may not need a barrier-free shower or an extra bedroom for live-in help today, but tomorrow may be another story. If you have older friends with special needs, ask them what design features they appreciate most.

spaces. The last problem—separating the bedroom from the living area—was solved by designing a freestanding console (facing page) large enough to hold all of Julie's clothes and high enough to block sightlines from the main house, yet low enough to allow afternoon sun to reach the back wall.

Installing remotely operable windows in the bedroom walls took a bit of advance planning because the system had two principal electrical components: a bank of controllers (hidden in one of the closets) that respond to a wireless remote control, and a small electric motor for each window. The motors are after-market items that don't come with the windows, but virtually any building-supply center that sells windows can order them. The motors work with most crank-operated windows. After removing the crank, you slide the motor housing onto the splined shaft that holds it. Overall, it's a simple, cost-effective solution for increasing ventilation where high ceilings or limited user mobility preclude hand-cranking windows open and shut.

Placing remote-operable windows high on bedroom walls creates privacy without sacrificing natural light.

The custom-made bamboo console separates the bedroom from public areas but doesn't block the afternoon sun. High ceilings increase the volume of the in-law and give it an expansive feeling. Radiant heating embedded in the concrete floors keeps things warm and cozy year-round.

GREEN TOUCHES

Because Julie's in-law was the first green residence in her community, she wanted it to excite and inspire her neighbors. A great example of urban infill and compact living, its green profile includes:

- Energy-efficient lighting and appliances
- Bamboo-faced cabinets, reduced-formaldehyde plywood
- Radiant space heating and on-demand hot water system (a wall-hung tankless boiler serves both)
- Salvaged FSC-approved framing and finish lumber
- Zero-VOC paint throughout
- Recycled tiles on bathroom walls and floors
- A rainwater catchment system

The sun isn't the only thing that moves freely through Julie's place. There's not a stair, curb, or threshold anywhere and should Julie need wheelchair access in the years to come, all doors and passageways—including the shower doorway—are wide enough to roll into. The kitchen counter heights vary to accommodate different activities: most are set at a standard 36-in. height but the sewing counter in the corner is lower, perfect for someone sitting.

Comfortable as Julie's place is, though, it is not self-sufficient—and that's deliberate. Julie wanted her kin close so she could spend time with them. Although Julie's kitchen has a compact fridge/freezer, a cooktop with two burners, and a convection microwave, she takes most of her meals in the big house, where she and Denise split cooking duties. That's also where she does her laundry and stores most of her quilting stuff. In effect, the big house is shared space. Julie's place, on the other hand, is her castle. So when the kids get a bit wild before bedtime, Julie often calls it a day, kisses them good night, and says, "Okay, grandma's going home now." ☐

plans and permits

DEALING WITH TOWN PLANNING and building departments can be daunting. But once you get the hang of the language, procedures will become clearer, your confusion will abate, and the people you deal with will become, well, people. Even if you ultimately decide to have an architect or contractor manage your project, take the time to meet with a city planner and attend a public hearing or two. Those firsthand experiences will help you understand the issues and make better decisions. Who knows, you may even enjoy it.

This chapter will help you turn your ideas into plans, share

them with others, get them approved, and eventually get them built.

SEEING THE BIG PICTURE

Shepherding a project through any town or city bureaucracy is confusing, even if you do it for a living. The confusion comes, in part, from the plethora of titles used (they vary from town to town), the divisions within departments, and the increasing complexity of procedures. So let's simplify things a bit.

DOING THE TWO-STEP

Generally, getting something built is a two-step process that begins at Planning and ends at Building. (Note: Whenever you see Planning or Building capitalized in this chapter, it refers to departments.) In rural areas and small towns, these two departments may be combined, but usually they're separate: different issues, different bailiwicks, and different staff.

Planners are, first of all, the keepers of zoning regulations: how high a house may be or how big, how close it may be to neighboring houses, how much of a lot the house and ADU may cover, and what public processes you must go through to make changes to your existing property. In other words, Planning cares most about how a building looks and how its use affects the community.

The building department focuses on the construction and functioning of the house, including health and safety issues. They want to know how much steel is in the foundation, how the walls support the roof, what kind of insulation is in the walls, what sort of siding is on them, and so on. They're particularly interested in the details of plumbing, electrical, and heating systems.

CALL 'EM ADUS. Staffers in planning and building departments usually refer to an in-law unit as an ADU (accessory dwelling unit)—bureaucrats love acronyms. That's what we'll call them in this chapter (just so you can get accustomed to the lingo), and it's the term you should use when you meet with a planner.

The planning department oversees zoning regulations and how a dwelling looks. The building department specifies construction details.

They want to know the type and location of fire sprinklers. In other words, Building makes sure the ADU is constructed according to the building codes, and that it is safe to live in. A building inspector will visit the project at various points during construction just to make sure what's on the plans is what gets built.

CAN YOU RUN THE GAUNTLET?

Some municipal governments encourage homeowners who want to remodel their own homes or add an ADU. They clearly explain approval and permitting procedures, provide free handouts or online resources, and make staff available to answer questions. Now and then, they even streamline regulations and approval processes to encourage the creation of ADUs. Santa Cruz, California, for example, offers residents a choice of preapproved building plans for different ADU types. Choose one and, after an expedited review, you're ready to start building. The city has even helped homeowners line up low-interest loans.

Other towns are not so encouraging. For whatever reason, whether budget shortfalls or bureaucratic inertia, their planning and building departments are tough to navigate if you're not a building professional. Of course, homeowners have the right to manage their own projects, but it will be a long, hard slog to get things approved and built. In general, the bigger the city, the truer this is. In such circumstances, hiring a general contractor or architect may be the best way to go.

TALKING TO A PLANNER

You won't know how easy or difficult it is to create an ADU until you ask. The first step—visiting the city planning department—will be quite informative and won't cost anything more than a bit of your time. Planners spend most days reviewing

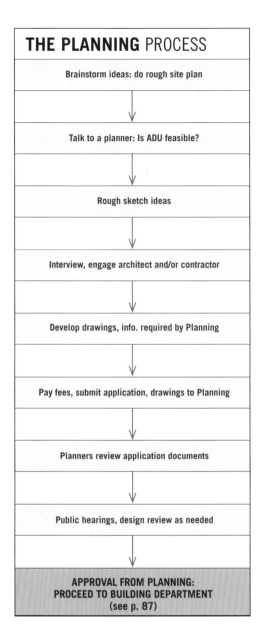

THE PLANNING PROCESS

Brainstorm ideas: do rough site plan

↓

Talk to a planner: Is ADU feasible?

↓

Rough sketch ideas

↓

Interview, engage architect and/or contractor

↓

Develop drawings, info. required by Planning

↓

Pay fees, submit application, drawings to Planning

↓

Planners review application documents

↓

Public hearings, design review as needed

↓

**APPROVAL FROM PLANNING:
PROCEED TO BUILDING DEPARTMENT**
(see p. 87)

projects for code compliance and many nights explaining code requirements at public hearings. Spend a half hour with a planner and you'll have a good idea if your ADU project is feasible. To get the most out of the meeting, do your homework first.

WHERE TO FIND A PLANNER

Chances are that the planning department's address and hours are posted on the city website or in the phone book. You can call to set up an appointment with a planner or just drop by the planning counter during weekdays. Drop-ins are handled on a first-come, first-serve basis. If you live in an unincorporated town and are unsure where to go, call the county planning department, give your address or AP number (assessor's parcel number on your property tax bill), and they'll tell you who has jurisdiction over your area.

WHAT TO BRING TO THE MEETING

The first step is an easy one: Get a planner on the phone, tell him that you're thinking about adding an ADU, and go from there. If he says, "not allowed in this town," then that's that. But if he says they're sometimes allowed, make an appointment to go in for a talk to find out more. You don't *have* to bring anything to that meeting. But if you take a rough site plan (a sketch of your property with your house on it) and the proposed changes you'd like to make—and a list of questions—a planner will probably be able to give you a good sense of what's possible. Of course, the planning department will have accurate site plans for the entire town and can pinpoint your property easily. But if you want to save an extra trip into the planning department, or if you just want to get an idea of how your project might fit into the neighborhood, make some sketches.

Site plan. To create a site plan, enter your street address into Google Maps, zoom in to choose the closest view, click the "satellite" button, and then print out the aerial view of your house and the houses around you. Trees may obscure some of the buildings so, to simplify things, put tracing paper over the photo, completely outline each building, and use broken lines to indicate fences or your property lines. Be as accurate as you can, but don't agonize.

House location. Once you have a site plan, indicate where you think your ADU

might go by drawing a little rectangle on your site plan to indicate it (ideally, at the same scale as your site plan). You should have a rough idea where the ADU's entrance and windows will be, but don't include interior walls and all that. Planners don't care about the inside of the building. You're adding the ADU's footprint to the site plan only to show how the ADU relates to the house, property lines, and neighboring houses.

Elevations. If you enjoy drawing, do a few elevations, too. Google's street view will give you the front elevation of the existing house, so if your ADU is around the side or in the back, walk around the house and snap photos with a digital camera. Load the photos into your computer, print them up on plain paper, and sketch ADU side and front views onto the photos, indicating the location of windows and the door(s). Take a few photos of your yard and neighboring houses, too—they may be food for thought and conversation when you and the planner talk.

Using a printout of a Google satellite map of your neighborhood, you can quickly create a rough site plan of your property. Site plans help planners envision the location and approximate size of your in-law unit.

WHAT TO ASK THE PLANNER

In addition to seeing if your ADU is feasible, ask about specifics such as height, setbacks, size limitations, and parking requirements. There may also be detailed requirements relating to such features as slide zones, creek setbacks, and seismic zones. If any zoning issue is a deal-breaker in your town, you need to know about it before you commit to a particular ADU plan or spend a lot of money on architect's drawings. Planners will freely identify contentious issues, though they won't suggest how to resolve them.

Some zoning issues will trigger a higher level of review—usually called a public hearing or design review. Although the decision to schedule a public hearing will not be made until you formally submit an application, ask the planner if a public hearing seems likely for your ADU. Public hearings are nothing to fear, but they typically prolong the approval process and call for you to explain your project to a board of zoning commissioners.

At the end of your meeting, the planner will probably give you a summary of town zoning requirements, as well as a "submittal checklist" of documents you'll need to gather should you decide to submit a formal application.

WHO DO YOU CALL?

After talking with the planner and looking over the planning checklist, take some time to consider your next steps. If you are converting existing rooms into an ADU and there are few or no structural changes required—as sometimes happens with carve-outs or basement conversions—you

Many municipal planning departments have design reviews to make sure that new projects are visually compatible with the neighborhood.

might be able to do all the design and most or all of the construction. If, on the other hand, your project is complex or raises zoning issues likely to trigger a public hearing, working with an architect and a general contractor (GC) will be very helpful.

SOME ASSEMBLY REQUIRED

Building and remodeling projects can get complicated and expensive. Whether you run the whole show, from planning to construction, or you turn the entire thing over to a professional has a lot to do with how much time, expertise, and money you have. If you don't have a ton of money, you might want to get involved in as many places as you can to save some of it. But if you can afford it, it might make more sense just to hire an architect and let him or her find a good general contractor. Assembling the right team will make the rest of the project go smoothly. Maybe you can do it. Maybe you can't.

It could be that you have a relative who's a contractor so that's who you choose first. Or maybe you're keen on a GC who did another project for you. In that case, you may want to ask the GC for the names of an architect he enjoys working with. Or maybe you know an architect but no contractors. In that case, rely on the architect to find the rest of the team.

So, as far as assembling a team to help you get the job done, here's the bottom line: Make sure they are people who can see eye to eye with you and who will work well together. Often, the best teams are ones who have worked together before. The worst thing you can do is bring in a GC long after the plans are all complete, you're in a hurry to get started, and you only have a vague understanding of what kind of person he is and what quality of work he does. You can hope it will work out, but that's a recipe for disaster.

CONTRACTS

If you hire both an architect and a contractor, each will probably need a separate contract with you. The contractor draws up the construction contract because he's most conversant with those issues. If there's an architect involved, often they'll use the standard AIA (American Institute of Architects) contract. There are short forms for cost plus a fee, percentage fee, or a straight bid. Many contractors don't like to use the AIA contract because it puts the architect in the middle—administering the contract, approving of change orders, and so on. However you sort things out, have your lawyer review any contract before you sign it.

ARCHITECTS AND ADUS

An architect can refine your design ideas and draw up the floor plans and elevations needed for the submittal set. But an architect can do much more. He or she will devise solutions that maximize natural light and usable space—always a challenge in small ADUs—and suggest materials and appliances that are stylish, functional, and energy-conserving. An architect can also assemble a team of specialists as needed, from energy specialists to structural engineers.

As important, a perceptive architect can steer your project through the trickier parts of the approval process. Given enough time, perhaps you could create a set of construction documents on your own. But getting a project approved and built is a hardball game. If your first submittal set isn't accurate, complete, and professional looking, it will be viewed with skepticism and greater scrutiny. To quote a seasoned contractor, "Your documents must not only explain clearly what you want to do, but explain it in the way that planners want to hear it."

A good architect may also be invaluable in presenting your ADU to neighbors and, if need be, to planning commissioners at

This custom-built cottage was rolled to the site on a trailer. In fact, it still sits on a trailer in case the owner wants to move to another location. Off-site construction also reduces the impact on the neighbors.

a public hearing. Many architects will happily manage the construction phase as well (for an extra fee), but, more often than not, that's the purview of the general contractor.

ENTER THE GC

To save money, homeowners sometimes act as their own general contractor for a while. At first glance, obtaining ("pulling") permits, ordering materials, hiring sub-contractors, and calling for inspections doesn't seem so difficult. Well, it is. For one thing, how quickly a sub returns your call often depends on how long he's known you, and as a homeowner, you probably don't know many subs. And if, for what-ever reason, you can't keep the subs, materials, and inspections flowing in the proper sequence, your project can seize up in a big hurry.

GCs have mastered the complicated art of maneuvering and managing—or at least the ones who stay in business do. If your project is simple, maybe you can manage it. But if your ADU is at all complicated or if you're not well organized, patient, very persistent, and have plenty of time to do what has to be done, hire a general contractor who is. Contractors with some architectural training may offer "design-build" services under one roof—or in one person.

There are many ways to find a good GC. Start with the recommendations of friends who've recently completed an ADU or a remodel. Architects will also know who's good. Once you have two or three names, call each one up, ask for an hour of his or her time to look at schematics of your

TRUST BUT VERIFY. Licensed contractors must have insurance policies that cover themselves and anyone working for them. Before work begins, ask to see your contractor's proof of insurance. Homeowners are ultimately responsible for what happens on their property, so an uninsured contractor who gets injured may put your financial health at risk.

ADU, and get an idea of what it might cost. Most builders won't want to ballpark a final price based on a schematic, but they will give you a price range per sq. ft. based upon construction costs in your area. In any event, if you find a contractor you like, ask for references and a list of jobs she or he is proud of.

A MEETING OF MINDS

As soon as there are several schematics to look at, get your architect and contractor in a room together to troubleshoot them. That will often yield a healthy mix of blue-sky solutions and down-to-earth pragmatism. If, for example, you're weighing a bump-out versus a detached unit, the contractor might have concrete reasons for choosing one or the other. He might say, for example, "It's going to be a lot easier to do a detached unit because this bump-out will have to tie into some

tricky roof framing and will probably interfere with its venting." Or maybe he'll say, "Bumping out will be much cheaper because we already have one wall and it will be easy to work with."

SUBMITTING YOUR APPLICATION TO PLANNING

The information that must be submitted when applying for a permit to build an ADU—*the submittal set*—is spelled out in the checklist or guidelines you received from the planning department; the list is probably also available on the town website. Follow it closely.

SUBMITTAL SET ELEMENTS

Generally, submittal sets include a set of *design development drawings*, elevations, a site plan, and a brief, written project description. Design development drawings must contain accurate overall dimensions,

Any successful in-law project requires the close collaboration of designers, builders, and homeowners.

and their elevations should have windows and doors correctly sized and located. In other words, they are a set of technical drawings that accurately show what the ADU is going to look like but not how it's going to be built. On the other hand, *working drawings* have all the information needed to build every detail. The site plan should show the house and ADU, and their relationships to property lines and other houses. And of course the height should be accurate.

REQUESTING A VARIANCE

When some aspect of your project violates a city-zoning requirement, you can seek a "variance"—in effect, permission to break the requirement. Some zoning issues are not hard and fast. If you're not allowed to block a neighbor's view, for example, how do you define "block"? A quarter of the view? Half? If they can still see the mountains but just not as much of them, have you diminished the value of their property?

One generally effective argument is to point out that other people in the neighborhood have structures that violate the same rule or regulation to which you're seeking a variance. And that you have certain rights as a homeowner that can't reasonably be denied. If every house in your neighborhood has an addition but yours doesn't, you can argue that you have a right to add on even though your lot is small. (See the case study on p. 183.) Likewise, if you can't build right or build left because of setback restrictions, you may have a reasonable case for building up.

One of the reasons this argument is compelling is that most towns have buildings that are "nonconforming"; that is, they don't meet zoning requirements but are allowed because they were built before codes were enacted. Making changes to nonconforming buildings often calls for creative design. A garage that's been sitting on a property line for 50 years might be turned into an ADU, for example, though Planning may make you jump through hoops to convert it. Even if the building is about to fall down, you may be still able to "grandfather" it if you leave an original wall or a roof intact and remodel around it. (See Case Study 22 on p. 188.) Generally, you can renovate a grandfathered structure as long as you stay within its existing footprint, but if you want to make it bigger, wider, or taller, you'll need a variance.

The drawings you submit may not have every detail, but what is there must be accurate. If you have a public hearing, the zoning board is going to base its decision upon what you've given them. If the hearing becomes contentious and you deviate at all from what they've approved—say, you want to add a bigger window facing the street or a larger door—such changes may require another hearing. So try to get it right the first time.

Again, follow the guidelines. Some towns may require a building cross section. Others may ask for shadow studies to see if your ADU will put adjacent properties in shade. In general, don't submit anything more than what's asked for and especially don't give specifics about the unit's interior finish details. Planners don't care about what kind of cabinets you install or what floor finishes you use. After you get zoning approval, you will be free to make almost any interior changes you want, including structural ones, as long as they don't change the exterior of the building.

NEXT STEPS

After you submit your application and the submittal set, the staff of the planning department will analyze your plans. They usually have 30 days to tell you if your drawings are complete, during which period they might send out copies to various agencies, such as the fire department, the water district, public works, health and safety, the urban forester, environmental agencies, and so on. The fire department may say, for example, this ADU must have sprinklers. The urban forester may object that the proposed project will damage specimen trees the town is trying to protect. Every agency may come back with requirements or comments, which Planning will summarize and bring to your attention. They may ask for more documents.

Once project plans are considered complete (all comments have been received from agencies and you've changed your submittal set accordingly), you will get an official notice if a public hearing is required. Planning will set a hearing date, usually several weeks in advance, and send out notices to contiguous neighbors and, many times, to every neighbor within a given distance of the project. (In some towns, the applicant is required to send out notices; many companies specialize in this service.) You may also be required to post notices of your proposed project around the neighborhood.

You may even have to erect story poles (poles at the ridges and eaves) to show where the ADU will be located, how high it will rise, how it will impact neighboring views, and so on. Some towns will even ask you to connect poles with taut string or lumber to indicate the ridge of the new roof, or have a surveyor confirm that your poles are accurate.

RALLYING THE NEIGHBORS

Once you know your project is going to a public hearing, launch your charm offensive. Human beings do not like change. So as best you can, try to lessen that fear and you'll be more successful. And nothing succeeds like the personal touch. Show neighbors sketches early on and as you do so, be upbeat and empathetic. Show them that as you developed your ideas you were thinking of them: "We know you love to garden, so we pulled the building back so it wouldn't shade your roses." Or, "All the windows on this side of the in-law unit are either

Adding a rental unit (at left) improved the visual proportions of the main house, while minimally impacting the site or the Seattle neighborhood.

TO WIN OVER THE NEIGHBORS, have an open house in which you lay out drawings of your in-law unit; have your architect on hand to answer questions. Put out a little wine and cheese, too. People tend to complain less when there's a party going on.

obscure or way above eye level because we didn't want to impact your privacy."

Put yourself in your neighbors' shoes. Listen to what they have to say and be sensitive to their concerns. Don't wait until the design is already done—let them know you're willing to work with them. And if one set of neighbors is particularly contentious, approach them early and show them what you're doing. It takes a bit of courage to go into the lion's den but even if you don't convince them, it's important to try. When the public hearing rolls round, if you have most of the neighbors supporting you and one person grousing about the project, the zoning commissioners will be less likely to listen to that person—especially if he lives four doors down and only sees your house as he drives by.

One last piece of advice. You may have heartfelt reasons for creating an ADU, but telling them to a staffer at the planning counter or to zoning commissioners in a

public hearing is unlikely to sway them. Far better to tell your neighbors what this project means to you—whether it's the chance to care for an elderly parent or the extra income you need to stay in the house and neighborhood you love—and have them voice your reasons at the public hearing. It will be far more compelling coming from a neighbor.

GETTING APPROVAL

For most towns, zoning approval takes place in one of three ways: (1) a staff person in the planning department grants an administrative approval without a hearing; (2) there's a public hearing and zoning commissioners issue recommendations; or (3) there is an appeal that the town council decides. How your project is approved will depend on its scope, how closely it conforms to zoning requirements, and town politics. In some towns, everything goes to a public hearing.

If your ADU or remodel (right) matches an architectural style that's already there (below), your project is more likely to be approved quickly.

ADMINISTRATIVE APPROVAL

In general, if your project is minor or it complies with zoning ordinances and use-conditions (such as whether you create an ADU to generate income or to house a family member), your approval will be granted quickly, without a public hearing, and a *zoning certificate* will be issued. At that point, you can usually apply for a building permit. (Again, this isn't true for all towns. If it looks like a public hearing isn't required for your project, try to get something in writing from a planner that your project is "good to go" before you develop working drawings.)

If your project is compliant but town procedures require a hearing anyway, the project will often be consigned to a *consent calendar.* Such hearings are usually held during the day when few people are likely to attend, and after cursory discussion the project is approved. (You aren't required to attend, but it's a good idea to go, in case there is an unexpected objection at the last moment.) After the hearing, Planning sends out notices of tentative approval to neighbors, which may trigger objections or more hearings, but that's rare. Usually, the project just proceeds to its building permit phase.

PUBLIC HEARINGS AND APPEALS

If your project is extensive, zoning is strict, or neighbors raise objections, there will be a full public hearing after your plans have been reviewed. At the hearing, a planner presents the project, the applicants or their architect defends it, and neighbors express their support or objections. Then the zoning commissioners deliberate and rule on the project. Four categories of people typically participate in a public hearing:

- **A planning staff person** is always present. Typically, the person received

ATTENDING A PUBLIC HEARING is a great eye-opener and good fun when it's not your project that's being discussed. It will show what kinds of issues are likely to emerge and maybe even how—or how not—to answer them.

your plans and checked them for completeness.

- **Homeowners and their representative,** whether an architect or general contractor.
- **A board of zoning commissioners** (also called planning commissioners) is usually five to seven appointed or elected people. The commissioners hear the facts presented by the staff and architect or homeowner, and weigh the opinions expressed by the public. They ultimately make the decision.
- **The general public.** Meetings are posted publicly and all neighbors within a given distance receive notice of the hearing sent by the planning department.

A typical hearing

The planning staffer will present the project and describe its impact. After his or her presentation, the staffer usually makes a recommendation for approval or disapproval. After that, the homeowner (or his architect) will have a chance to

Progressive cities such as Portland, Oregon, encourage smart growth. After winning a citywide competition, this 15-ft.-wide masterpiece of urban infill was one of two designs the city chose to offer as permit-ready plans.

further describe or, if necessary, to defend the project. You might provide color renderings or specialty plans or maybe even a scale model to explain what the project will look like and how it will fit in.

After that, any neighbor can speak for or against your project. There may be an opportunity for you or your architect to respond or to clarify a disputed issue. Then the commissioners will close the meeting to further public comment and discuss the merits (and demerits) of the project. Though the public is allowed to listen, they must remain silent. When deliberations are done, the commissioners might approve the project, reject

it, continue discussion to the next meeting, or suggest design compromises to offset noncomplying elements.

If your application is approved, a planner will send you a letter listing any conditions that the commissioners recommended or that codes require (see the sidebar on the facing page). After the hearing, there's a brief appeal period. If no one appeals, you can apply for a building permit.

If your application is rejected, you can appeal to the city council, though the outcome can depend on many intangibles, including political clout. If the town or city council says no then that's the end of the line. But if you can't get the ADU you want within current codes, you can always get involved, rally the neighbors, elect commissioners, and change the laws. It happens more often than you think. In fact, Santa Cruz's model ADU program grew out of such citizen advocacy. And there's a sweet story about how it happened (see p. 90).

ON TO THE BUILDING DEPARTMENT

You did it. You completed the first leg of the design process when you received approval from the planning department. As you and your team create a submittal set with working drawings for the building department, you're in the home stretch. When this set of documents is approved, you'll receive a building permit and a green light to start working on your ADU.

CREATING A SUBMITTAL SET

From the building department or the city website, get a guideline that lists the mandatory elements of a submittal set for a building permit. At this point, your architect and general contractor will go into high gear as they begin creating working drawings, the final set of drawings from which contractors will work.

This stage is all about details. If there's a structural component (an augmented or new foundation, seismic retrofitting, etc.) to your ADU, the drawing sets approved by Planning will now be reviewed by a structural engineer. Sets will also be sent to electrical, plumbing, and HVAC (heating, ventilation, and air-conditioning) subcontractors so each can make suggestions and prepare their bids. There may also be soil engineers involved and, most certainly, energy consultants. (Typically, in a small project, the architect assembles most of this information, and the appropriate subcontractor often works out unresolved details on-site.) At this

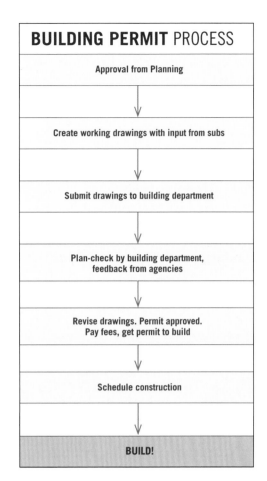

BUILDING PERMIT PROCESS

Approval from Planning

↓

Create working drawings with input from subs

↓

Submit drawings to building department

↓

Plan-check by building department, feedback from agencies

↓

Revise drawings. Permit approved. Pay fees, get permit to build

↓

Schedule construction

↓

BUILD!

"APPROVED ON THESE CONDITIONS . . ."

The approval you receive after a public hearing is often called a *conditional approval*. In fact, almost all zoning approvals are conditional: some towns list 40 conditions that must be met. The zoning commissioners, for example, may have approved your ADU on the condition that you modify its height or increase its setback from a property line. Or, in response to neighborhood concerns about noise, they may have limited the hours of construction or required that you develop a traffic management plan to deal with big trucks.

There may also be conditions on the use and sale of your property if you create an ADU. If you're not allowed to sell the property as two units, for example, you may have to de-convert it before selling. And codes usually require that the owner must live on the premises if there's an ADU. Take these conditions seriously. A planner will scrutinize later documents such as building permits to make sure all the agreed-to conditions have been incorporated.

point, there is a lot of back-and-forth between the subs, the architect, and the general contractor. The structural engineer, for example, may suggest foundation details but the architect or general contractor might challenge them because of their cost, and propose alternatives.

SUBMITTING THE DOCUMENTS

Once your team has heard back from all the subs and specialists and incorporated their suggestions, it will review once more all the items on the building department's checklist. That done, four sets of working drawings and supporting documents will be printed, someone will write a check to cover the cost of checking the plans and then the whole package will be submitted to the building department.

Generally, it takes the building department three or four weeks to check the plans but it could take as long as three months. The building department routes your plans to other agencies that may have seen them at the earlier go-round; at this point, they're checking to make sure you complied with their earlier requests. They'll send a set back to Planning, too.

Once this review process is complete, Building will either stamp your plans and say, "Here's your building permit," or tell you, "We have some issues you need to resolve." Their issues are typically construction details: changing a handrail height, showing a cross section of stair construction, or revising a structural calculation they don't like. In the old days, someone at the building department would just indicate corrections in red ink right on the plans and say, "Correct this and you'll get your permit." But today everything is by the book, so you will probably receive a letter containing comments. If there are issues to be addressed, you must respond to that letter item by item, redraft the plans showing exactly what changed, and resubmit. Usually the resubmittal goes to the same building department staffer and you'll get a quick reply.

Once the building permit is approved, it's time to go to work.

DO YOU NEED A PERMIT FOR SMALL STUFF?

Even when there's little construction involved in converting space to an ADU, always check local codes to see if you need a building permit. In general, you need a building permit for any work that involves structural changes such as wall framing, modifications to the outside of a building

Time to go to work! Replacing an undersized foundation is a good opportunity to develop the space underneath the house.

Adding a new electrical or plumbing fixture usually requires a building permit. Replacing an existing fixture usually doesn't.

such as adding windows or a new entrance, or work that could affect the health and safety of future occupants. Adding new electrical circuits or extending existing circuits requires a permit, as does plumbing work that involves adding or relocating pipes to serve fixtures in new locations. As a rule of thumb, you don't need a building permit if you replace a fixture such as a sink, toilet, or washing machine as long as you don't change existing pipes.

Replacing a water heater, however, requires a permit even if you connect the new water heater to existing pipes. Here, the issue is safety: Inspectors want to be sure that gas- and oil-fired water heaters are correctly vented and electric heaters are properly wired. They'll also check that temperature-and-pressure-relief (TPR) valves, which keep water heaters from exploding, are correctly rated and installed. □

BUSTED! A TRUE STORY

Many homeowners create in-laws that, though compliant with current building codes, are *outlaws* (illegal units) because a permit was never issued for construction. Stiff fees and red tape are the reasons most often given for not getting a permit. Owning an outlaw may cost you in other ways, however. Consider this example:

"I didn't get a permit because we milled the trees on our property and I didn't want to pay $2,500 for an 'expert' to tell me that it was good wood. We had just finished the cabin and installed the kitchen stove when a guy with a hardhat and a clipboard comes walking down the drive. I knew right away what it was about. He stood next to the cabin and said, 'Do you have an illegal building on this property?' And I said, 'You're looking at it.'

"So I had to go through the rigmarole of permitting after all. Because the cabin was built to code, the county didn't fine me much but the permitting fees were expensive. In the end, setting things right cost about $10K. So it cost about $30K to build the cabin and about a third more to get it permitted. I wasn't happy about spending that money. On the other hand, I'm home free now. I have nothing to hide.

"If I want to rent this place, I just put an ad in the paper. If there's a political dispute in town, I can stand up and speak my mind. Cutting corners and not getting permits is very common around here—a deck here, a little shed, a room that was storage but now is a bedroom—but not getting a permit makes you feel vulnerable. If your neighbors get miffed about your dog barking, they could turn you in.

"Incidentally, it wasn't a neighbor who called the county—my neighbors are all friends and, besides, I discussed the cabin with them before I built it—but someone in town had a beef with me. But initially I didn't know who had turned me in and that climate of suspicion can be very corrosive. In time, though, I got over it and moved on. So in hindsight, it was a valuable lesson."

CALL 811 BEFORE YOU DIG. This federally mandated program helps prevent damage to underground utility lines. Dial 811, give the operator the location of your project and within days someone from a local utility will visit and mark the location of utility lines. For more information, check the website (www.call811.com).

you can go home again

Herb and Ellie Foster's comfy old farmhouse in Santa Cruz was, in many ways, the heart of the neighborhood, and over the years it probably hosted more potlucks, community meetings, and teenagers hanging out than all the other houses on the block combined. So when their kids moved out and the stairs became too much for the couple to navigate, Herb and Ellie's first instinct was to figure out how to stay in the community they had lived in since 1958.

Seen from the street, this in-law cottage behind the main house is a good neighbor—modest in scale and architecturally compatible with surrounding homes.

Building an in-law cottage in the backyard had a lot of appeal: they could live in it and rent out the main house to offset taxes and defray the costs of maintaining their property. But when the Fosters visited the city planning department to see about building a legal second unit, they got a chilly reception. They learned that permit fees were formidable, zoning compliance was complicated, and they would have to submit to a public hearing. The city wanted to discourage second units. So in the end Herb and Ellie sold the house to their son David and moved into an apartment downtown.

CHANGING CITY HALL

David Foster knew how much his folks loved the old neighborhood. Trained as a housing planner, he also knew a few things about how city governments work. So when David and his wife Margo returned to Santa Cruz in the 1990s after a decade away, one of the first things they did was to help create a community group called Affordable Housing Advocates (AHA!) that addressed the city's acute housing shortage. One of the most cost-effective ways to increase affordable housing, according to the group, was for the city to revamp its zoning codes and encourage the creation of in-law units in single-family neighborhoods. As it educated and organized community members, the group met with city officials to find common ground.

Kobe Allen, Herb and Ellie's great-grandson, clearly relished his work.

In the decade since David's parents had tried to create an in-law unit, the climate at city hall had changed dramatically. Housing costs had spiked and cities across the country were struggling to provide affordable housing—especially for seniors and others with limited means. So city planners were now very receptive to grassroots solutions. It didn't happen overnight, but by 2003, the City of Santa Cruz had developed a model ADU program that liberalized its zoning codes, streamlined the permitting process, and actively assisted citizens who wanted to create an in-law unit on their property.

Not long after the city's new ordinances went into effect, David Foster applied for a permit to build a backyard cottage for his parents. After giving it a lot of thought, David and Margo decided to build a cottage partially of straw bales. The beauty and green profile of straw-bale construction appealed to them. Equally compelling was the chance to get the community involved in its construction—like a barn raising of old. First, they had to site the cottage and design it.

A MODEL IN-LAW

Older people often value their independence and fear becoming a burden, so they may have to be sold on moving into an in-law. Initially, Herb and Ellie resisted moving again, but their son, David, built a scale model of the straw-bale cottage, with a roof one could lift off so they could look inside. After three months of friends coming by their apartment and commenting favorably on the model, Herb and Ellie finally called David and said, "OK, count us in." After that, they showed up at the job site every day to watch the construction.

Herb and Ellie oversee construction of their in-law cottage.

Floor Plan

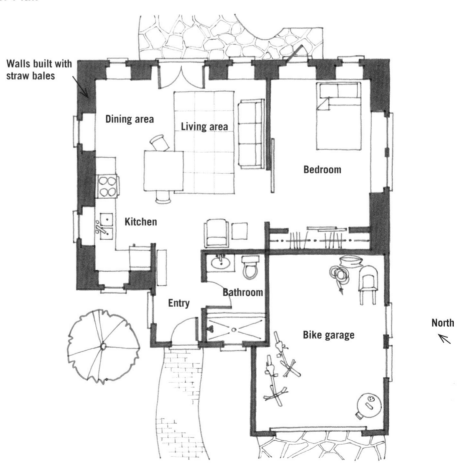

Walls built with straw bales

Dining area

Living area

Bedroom

Kitchen

Bathroom

Entry

Bike garage

North

FINDING COMMON GROUND

Siting an in-law cottage in the large garden near the house was a non-starter because that would have sacrificed a patch of loose, rich soil that had been tended for almost a century. Also, it would have diminished a neighbor's views and privacy. The back end of the lot was promising because it didn't have a well-established garden or neighbors close by, but given the elder Fosters' limited mobility, the site was just too far from the house and street.

The Fosters had briefly considered converting the garage into an in-law, but it was simply too far gone. If they tore the garage down and replaced it with a cottage, however, the site was perfect. It was accessible, close to the house, had nice views of the yard, and if the cottage footprint extended straight back, all the vegetable gardens could stay.

Because the site was landscaped to slope gently away from the straw-bale cottage, there's no need for ramps and railings. A patterned patio constructed from urbanite (recycled concrete) provides visual interest to the entry area.

URBANITE

Urbanite is recycled concrete—most often an old 2-in.- or 3-in.-thick driveway or sidewalk that's been busted up and removed. Any old concrete will do, but unreinforced concrete is best because it doesn't have rebar or steel mesh to cut through. Typically, large chunks are busted up and then re-cut with a concrete-cutting saw with carbide-teeth blades. It's noisy, dirty work. Most often, the urbanite is laid much as you'd lay a stone walkway, with wide joints to allow water to drain. But if you want to create a walk surface that's smooth enough for a walker or a wheelchair, take pains to carefully cut and closely fit the urbanite.

Carefully situated in the yard, the cottage has garden views on two sides. A patio built at ground level created a barrier-free entrance to the back of the house.

CREATING A NATURAL RAMP

Because the Fosters decided to build a straw-bale in-law cottage, solving the issues of drainage and accessibility became even more pressing on the low-lying site. (Water is the Achilles' heel of straw.) Raising the cottage wasn't viable because Herb and Ellie couldn't negotiate stairs and a long ramp would have been unsightly and consumed precious space. In the end, David's brother Ken, a landscaper, came up with a more complete solution. His idea was to raise and re-contour the land so the cottage would sit above the floodplain, and then gently slope the yard away from the cottage so that his parents wouldn't have to deal with steps. It was the best solution, though it turned out to be more complicated than it sounds.

As with any well-built home, the straw-bale cottage sat on a concrete foundation 8 in. above grade. After drainage around the foundation had been installed, Ken Foster added, compacted, and re-graded additional layers of gravel, sand, and soil to create a firm yet permeable surface. Atop this, he installed a sloping patio of *urbanite* (see the sidebar on p. 93). In this case, the joints were fitted closely so that someone in a walker or a wheelchair could roll over it easily. Leading from the entry is a brick walkway whose upper end is the same level as the cottage floor. The last piece of the puzzle—preventing water from seeping into the house—was solved by 30-in. roof overhangs and a drop-down threshold on the bottom of the door.

WITHIN THE WALLS

Once the Fosters had figured out where and how to site the cottage, they turned their attention to designing its 640 sq. ft. of living space, the most allowed by the city for an ADU.

For stand-alone units, the city required that the main entrance face the street. (Placing an entrance toward the street also reduces the foot traffic between houses, which could disturb neighbors.) There was just enough room on the front (west) side to squeeze in a bathroom between the entry door and the garage. A bathroom close to the front door can be reached quickly by someone sitting outside.

There's very little space wasted on hallways or circulation. To reduce the distance that Herb and Ellie had to carry groceries, for example, the kitchen is the next closest room to the main entry. And the sliding door between the bedroom and the living room doesn't require room to swing out, so it saves space. All door openings are wide enough for someone using a walker or wheelchair or, if need be, wide enough for two people walking abreast. Finally, the living-dining room can accommodate two people or twenty simply by moving a table or pulling up a chair or two.

In the end, it all worked. And so, one summer morning in 2006, surrounded by family and a few neighbors who happened by, Herb and Ellie Foster came home for good. □

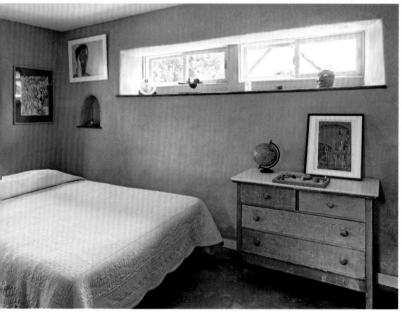

LEFT: Straw-bale buildings have wide, sculpted sills. This window was placed high to provide privacy for both the bedroom and the house next door.

ABOVE: This high-ceilinged living room can comfortably host a big family. And thanks to concrete floors with radiant heating, anyone can go barefoot year-round.

RIGHT: Four generations of Fosters. Herb and Ellie Foster's personal odyssey and the organizational skills of their son David (back row, right) helped spark the most progressive update of ADU zoning codes in the country.

CHAPTER 5

basement
in-law units

BASEMENT CONVERSIONS ARE A SMART, cost-effective way to add an in-law unit as long as there's enough headroom in the existing basement (see p. 24). And if your house sits on a sloping lot, all the better. The downhill wall of a basement is a great place to add large windows and French doors to maximize natural light and ventilation. The taller the windows and doors, the further inside sunlight can reach.

The one-level arrangement of a basement suite is especially appealing to someone with mobility problems or anyone who enjoys views of a yard or garden. To make coming and going even easier, you may want to place the tenant's parking spaces close to the basement entrance. Adding a patio with permeable materials will give the ground a drink when it rains, limit the amount of dirt tracked inside, and, in nice weather, create a pleasant space to sit and sun.

colors of a distant land

I t's not surprising that the Rutherfords' home is infused with the colors and crafts of Latin America. Dean, a contractor, was for a time a seminarian who worked with poor families in Mexico and Chile. Marty, an artist, began exploring Mexican art, music, and dance when she was seven. Downstairs, their in-law unit glows with the same spirit.

SEEING WHAT'S POSSIBLE

When Marty and Dean first saw the house in 1992, *glows* was probably not the first word that came to mind. The widow of the man who built the house in 1929 lived upstairs with four Dobermans, a goat, and a duck. Her

ABOVE: Constructed by an owner-builder in 1929, this house in the Berkeley Hills was in poor condition prior to being renovated in 1992. A year-round stream ran through the basement, making it uninhabitable. The original rental unit, located behind the garage, was in worse shape.

With the addition of an extensive drainage system and a new foundation, the house now sits high and dry. The gate at lower right leads to the renovated basement in-law unit.

living room ceiling was painted black. In the basement, a year-round stream ran through what had once been a rental unit behind the garage. As dark, dank, and dreary as the house was, however, the Rutherfords saw what it could become. They bought it.

Water was damming against the uphill side of the foundation and causing many of the problems in the basement, so the first order of business was to install extensive drainage pipes to route the flow away from the building. That done, Dean replaced the sections of foundation that had failed and then gutted the interior downstairs, removing truckloads of moldy drywall and any framing that was rotted or insect-infested. At this point, it was clear how to proceed with the basement. The greatest source of natural light was to the east, so Dean added a window and French doors to the back room. Then he framed out a new bedroom from a windowless corner of the garage. In addition to the fully

Alive with the colors of Latin America, the bedroom seems sunny even on a cloudy day. Decorative tiles serve as door and baseboard trim and dress up risers on the stairs leading to the floors above.

Floor Plan

Bath

Living/dining area

French doors

Future kitchenette

Double closet

Patio

Up

Bedroom

Laundry (unheated, unfinished space)

Existing garage

North ↑

With fully glazed doors facing east, the in-law gets plenty of natural light. To minimize maintenance and save water, the lushly planted yard is on a timed drip system.

glazed door and a large window in that new room, he also enlarged windows on the north wall.

The old bathroom was a primitive affair with cheap plastic fixtures that had to be gutted, but Dean kept it in the same location. Next came a laundry between the stairs to the first floor and the garage. It was not settled yet how the downstairs would be used, but Dean knew that if they ever wanted to rent it out, it would need a kitchen. But where? One afternoon while he was standing in the hallway next to the stairs, looking at the stand of plumbing pipes running to the floor above, inspiration struck (see the sidebar on p. 101).

CREATING A REFUGE

Once the basement was closed in—new doors and windows installed, walls insulated, and ceilings fitted with fiberglass batts to reduce sound transmission—Dean needed to turn his attention to the upstairs. He and Marty did much of the renovation themselves, when they had time and money. So it was several years before the basement unit was fully finished. That was fine because it allowed Dean to take his time with the tile work, which he loves doing.

But eventually the in-law unit came together and became a refuge for some of the people in Dean and Marty's lives. The first to live downstairs

Because this north-facing bathroom is the darkest part of the in-law, it got the most vivid colors. Marty, an artist, and Dean, a contractor, did most of the work themselves.

RUSTIC TILES SUCH AS *TALAVERA* TILES are often not flat and so require a bit more care when laying them. To forestall cracking, back-butter the tiles with thin-set mortar to fill high spots before placing the tiles in the thin-set layer on the floor.

were a series of college students from Mexico, Chile, and Brazil. They were like big sisters to the Rutherfords' daughter, Sarah, as she grew up. After that, Sarah lived downstairs for a time. In recent years, the in-law has been a temporary refuge for male friends who needed time to sort things out when their marriages were on the rocks. These days it's kind of a pit stop for South American shamans who come through and spend a couple weeks at a time. *Mi casa es su casa.*

At some future time, the Rutherfords may transform the present laundry into a kitchen because it's a bigger space. But short term, the kitchenette was consigned to the basement hallway because all the pipes are in the hallway wall, and because a hallway kitchen would be closer to the dining area. Usually the in-law unit's guests—even long-term ones—just use the upstairs kitchen anyway. The laundry area is funky and unfinished, so it makes a good mudroom and a convenient place to clean up after working in the garage. □

Sarah, Dean, Marty, Darrell, and their friend Ovidio share a laugh upstairs. The Rutherfords were in no rush to install the in-law unit's kitchen because sharing meals was a good opportunity to hang out with friends.

GETTING READY FOR A FUTURE KITCHEN

If you're not quite ready to install a kitchen, several preparatory steps done beforehand will make the installation easier later on. In the Rutherford house, all the plumbing for the upstairs floors—supply and DWV pipes—was clustered in a single wall. Before closing in that wall with drywall, Dean added tee fittings and *stub-outs* (short lengths of pipe) to accommodate a future kitchen sink. Because the basement was about to get a new concrete floor, he also stubbed out a 2-in. drain that ran under the stairway and connected to a drain in the laundry. Finally, he installed electrical outlet boxes for a compact refrigerator, electric range, and a microwave. The microwave, located over the range, would have an exhaust fan in its underside and so double as a range hood. The exhaust would attach to a 4-in. duct pipe that vented to an outside wall. Once this prep work was done, installing a kitchenette later on would be straightforward.

The louvered doors at left conceal a laundry closet now, but the space is fully wired, plumbed, and vented for a future compact kitchenette. At right is the door to the living-dining area.

one house, two yards

Pat and Chris Bear are therapists who pride themselves on seeing all sides of a story. They had also been renters for most of their lives so when they began renovating their new house and its basement in-law, it was second nature for them to consider their tenant's point of view. The completed project proves that nicely (see the photo below). At the time, however, they had no tenant and not much of an in-law.

After the house was lifted to increase ceiling height downstairs, the longer front stairs became a dramatic approach. Stair balusters and fence pickets have the same varied widths and rhythm.

Floor Plan

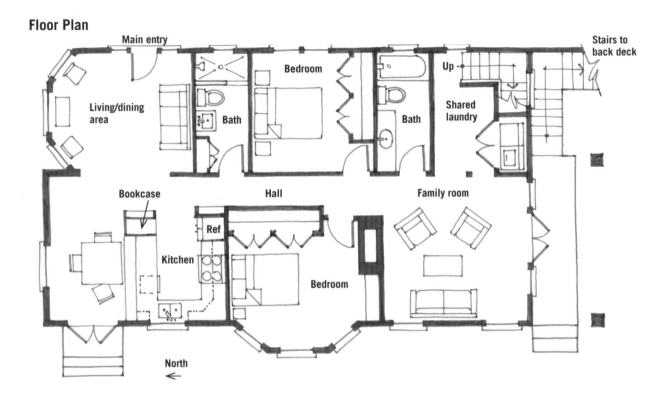

Main entry

Stairs to back deck

Living/dining area

Bath

Bedroom

Bath

Up

Shared laundry

Bookcase

Hall

Family room

Ref

Kitchen

Bedroom

North
←

ROOM FOR IMPROVEMENT

According to neighbors, the Victorian bungalow's basement had been rented for at least 40 or 50 years, mostly to single men. The "unit" was grim, with one middling room, one door, one window, one or two electrical outlets, and a modicum of plumbing. The basement flooded periodically and the foundation was in questionable condition.

On the upside, there was room for improvement: 1,300 sq. ft. of livable space could be gained if the Bears raised the house. They hired an architect to work up a set of plans, with only two criteria: the space had to be flexible and it had to be nice. The couple had no desire to be slumlords. After promising rough sketches in a month, the architect suggested that, in the meantime, Pat and Chris think about how best to share the yard areas with their tenant-to-be.

The house was a long box whose longest axis ran north to south on a corner lot in a quiet urban neighborhood. The main floor had a door at either end. The existing basement door faced west but, given the extent of the renovations, new doors could go anywhere except the north face. (Zoning regulations didn't allow entrances for both living spaces to face the street.) Pat and Chris wanted, above all, to be fair. Each unit should have decent sun, a yard of its own, and privacy. Because the front (north) yard faced the street and could have only one entrance, they decided to make it a common, decorative yard not really used by anyone. Surrounded by a low fence, it would show off the house's restored façade. The east face was the most problematic because the neighboring house was close and the yard got sun for only a few hours in the morning. To preserve privacy for both houses, not much could be done with that side of the building.

SECRETS OF A BELLYBAND

The wide horizontal *bellyband* midway up the exterior wall (see the photo on p. 104) allowed builders to strip the siding, access the framing, and raise the house without needing to replace all the siding above. The bellyband also hid the difference in wall thicknesses after the bottom was sheathed with plywood to create a shear wall (a rigid wall engineered to resist seismic forces). The siding of older houses in temperate climates was often nailed directly to the wall studs.

The prime spaces, then, faced west and south. The west yard, which ran along the length of the building, was by far the largest. With a 5-ft.- or 6-ft.-high fence to screen it from the street, it could be private and still get good afternoon sun. The architect would likely add many basement windows facing west, so that yard was the logical one to assign to the in-law. Problem was that arrangement was almost unfair to Chris and Pat because the remaining (south) yard, though sunny, was small. For several weeks, they agonized over what to do.

THEIR PLACE IN THE SUN

As it turned out, the architect had come to many of the same conclusions—plus one very welcome solution. The house had to be raised to create a comfortable ceiling height downstairs, she explained. What if they built exterior stairs on the south end to reach the newly elevated main floor and combined it with a deck? The deck would be sunny, large enough to entertain, and high enough to be private. It didn't take much convincing. Pat and Chris loved the idea of a yard but, true urbanites, decided to pass on mowing the grass.

The west yard. A salvaged fountain lends a peaceful, historical touch to the patio and entrance for the downstairs unit. The recycled brick patio, set in sand, is effortless to maintain and semi-permeable so rain won't pool.

A raised deck supplements a small backyard facing south, providing a sunny private space for the owners upstairs.

AIRY STAIRS

Elevated decks and exterior stairs needn't block the sun or feel oppressive to people living below. Consider these strategies:

- **Heighten up to lighten up.** If you build the deck high enough, sunlight will slant under it.

- **Think slender.** Use the smallest posts that can bear the load. In many cases, 4x4s will suffice but have an engineer determine what will work.

- **Skip the risers.** Stairs without solid risers allow more light and air to get through.

- **Watch for windows.** Avoid placing exterior stairs in front of windows.

- **Use the layout to help.** If your tenant has his own yard and entrance, he won't need to hang out under a deck.

Because the neighbor to the east is quite close, the door on that side has frosted and stained glass to admit light while maintaining everyone's privacy.

It all works. There's plenty of sun to go around and the tenant has two private entrances and a brick patio (see the photos on pp. 104–105). As it turned out, their first tenant was an old friend who relocated from Texas, so things are relaxed. Thanks to the architect's flexible layout, everyone shares the laundry. All the main living spaces of the in-law are blessed with abundant natural light, and the relatively open plan makes the most of it. Even the bathroom seems bright and airy, thanks in part to light, reflective surfaces. □

Though the owners tried to maintain a historical feel to the project, they weren't slavish about it. The Craftsman-inspired hardware is repro and the low-cost cabinets are from IKEA.

FACING PAGE: The bathroom is a subtle blend of salvaged and reproduction plumbing and lighting fixtures, period tiles, wood trim, and accent color.

BELOW: A stepped half wall is high enough to hide kitchen clutter yet low enough to allow lots of light into the dining nook, which opens onto the patio in nice weather.

finding treasure in the basement

T he modest Victorian cottage had experienced several lives before Fran Halperin and Eric Christ bought it in 1987. According to local lore, it was originally a banana-ripening shack built around the turn of the century. It was moved to its present location sometime in the 1940s and given a basement. Somewhat later, the basement became a rental unit, although a rather dank, head-ducking one, given its 6-ft. 2-in. ceilings and the floodplain it sat on. Cracks in the concrete floor allowed ground water to percolate upward during heavy rains.

Fran, an architect, and Eric, a contractor, gave the house a few more lives. For six years, they lived in the basement while the main level served as the office for their growing design-build business. Then the office moved out and they moved up. Following that, various nephews lived downstairs. Finally, in 2004, after renovating the main level, Fran and Eric decided it was time to overhaul the in-law.

ADDING VISUAL WARMTH

Despite the scarcity of natural light, Fran and Eric found other ways to make the space warm and appealing. They selected cheerful wall colors, adorned the walls with art, and installed low-voltage track lighting to vary the mood. To make the radiant floors look less monolithic, Eric acid-washed the concrete with color and scored it with a diamond pattern, which limits cracking.

Floor Plan

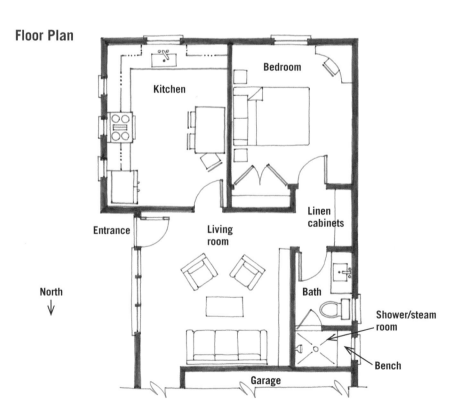

North ↓

Kitchen

Bedroom

Entrance

Living room

Linen cabinets

Bath

Shower/steam room

Bench

Garage

SITTING HIGH AND DRY

Built simply to raise the house above the floodplain, the basement was never meant to be a residence, hence the low ceilings. The first order of business was to raise and temporarily support the main house. Shortly after, the basement was gutted, the concrete slab was torn out, and an extensive drainage system was installed. The surface of the new slab was placed at least 1 ft. higher than the old one—well above the area's 100-year-base flood elevation.

That done, Eric and his crew framed the downstairs so the new in-law would have almost 9-ft. ceilings and plenty of light. In all, the new framing and foundation raised the house about 3½ ft., which provided a good opportunity to remove the ugly exterior stairs that served the main floor and replace them with an interior stairway.

The new floor plan also improved the in-law's entrance on the south-facing side of the house. Set into a recessed area whose overhang sheltered tenants from wet weather, the new entrance adjoined a patio. That south-facing wall was by far the best source of natural light, so Halperin designed a floor-to-ceiling window wall that transformed the basement into a garden apartment. Even the neighbors helped, however unintentionally: their facing windows were all high up, so the in-law's privacy was complete.

ABOVE LEFT: Originally, this Victorian featured ugly exterior stairs and a nonconforming basement rental with uncomfortably low ceilings. After extensive renovations, the house now has interior stairs, a new front entrance, and a cheerful downstairs suite with high ceilings and lots of light.

ABOVE RIGHT: The in-law suite's entrance is hidden from the street, tucked into a recessed area along the side of the house. The overhang shelters the entrance and creates privacy for the patio.

PRIVACY, COLOR, AND WARMTH

To make the most of the natural light, a large common room was created contiguous to the wall of windows (see the floor plan on p. 108). It could serve as a living room, library, or, were a tenant to work at home, an office. Right off the entrance door, to the southwest, was the most logical place for a kitchen because it looked out into the backyard. The bedroom is positioned in the northwest corner, farthest from the street and hence the most private location; it also has a view into the yard. The bathroom is placed near the bedroom, along the north wall, with built-in linen cabinets between the rooms. The bathroom's sole window is frosted to provide privacy from the neighboring house. Due to the long wall shared with the garage, there are no other windows along the north side.

An imbedded network of tubes containing fluid heated by a boiler warms the concrete floors. Radiant floors may well be the most efficient heating system because a radiant system heats objects, not air, and the heat is right where you want it: at your feet. If your floors are warm, you will be, too. Thanks to the south-facing windows, the floors probably absorb a bit of sunlight, especially in winter when the sun is low. Less well known is a concrete floor's ability to cool a space for long periods of time when the heat is off. Unless there is a very long hot spell, Fran and Eric's basement floors are always cool in the summer. □

The bedroom is located in the quietest corner of the basement, far from the street. Its only window looks out into the garden.

THE BATHROOM UP CLOSE

To compensate for its north-facing location, the bathroom features cool, light-colored glass tiles offset by an intense purple wall. The radiant floor is color-etched concrete; the countertop and other horizontal details are cast concrete, which was cast off-site and then installed. The 3-ft. by 5-ft. shower doubles as a mini-steam room with a concrete bench (not visible here) to relax on. To contain the moist air, glass panels run up to the sloped shower ceiling. When steam condenses on the ceiling, it runs down the walls rather than dripping onto bathers. The frosted hopper window can be left open to vent excess moisture without compromising security or privacy.

The bathroom shows a deft use of color and multi-functionality.

A south-facing wall of windows lets a lot of natural light into the space, while the low-voltage track system mounted to the ceiling allows tenants to spotlight art on the walls or deliver intense, focused light to selected work areas.

a basement aerie

A t first glance, Penny and James Tuer's in-law suite on Bowen Island is exotic for a basement apartment. The island is located in one of the most pristine bays in British Columbia—it's a fjord, actually—about 30 miles west of Vancouver. Situated on a rock outcrop high above Horseshoe Bay, the house has majestic outlooks, especially to the east.

Despite its colorful setting, however, it's still a basement unit. So anyone familiar with the tight spaces, limited headroom, and dark recesses under a house should appreciate this tale of turning an impossibly steep crawlspace into a handsome in-law suite with dramatic views.

The Tuer home is sort of a contemporary Craftsman, where cedar shingles and corrugated siding coexist and steel braces support large overhangs. Passive solar design also figures in the mix: concrete floors serve as thermal mass on the main floor while soundproofing the in-law below. Decks double as solar shades in the summer.

Floor Plan

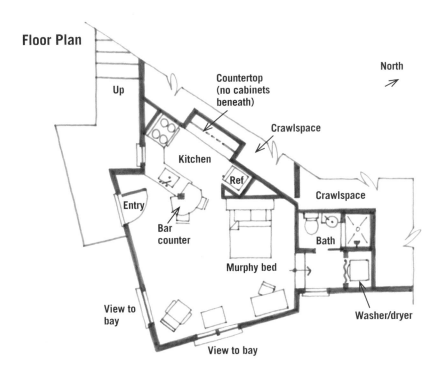

Up

Countertop
(no cabinets
beneath)

Crawlspace

North

Kitchen

Ref

Crawlspace

Entry

Bar
counter

Bath

Murphy bed

View to
bay

Washer/dryer

View to bay

USED AS THERMAL MASS, concrete floors absorb sunlight and slowly radiate it back into living spaces. Concrete is also ideal for muffling sound, making it a great soundproofing surface on the first floor if there's an in-law unit in the basement.

AN ACE IN THE HOLE

Building the house began in spring, 2004. Creating an in-law unit wasn't part of the original plan, but once James designed the foundation for the steeply sloping site and saw how much space was available under the living room, an in-law became an option. Hedging their bets, the Tuers ran rough plumbing and electrical lines down into the basement, and then added oversize window headers to the exterior walls. Whatever the size or location of future windows, they reasoned, adding them later would be easy.

Those decisions paid off handsomely the following January when the Tuers, then living in the States, abruptly decided to return to Bowen Island, launch an architectural practice, and await the birth of a baby girl. "We were in a mad panic about where we would live," James recalled. "We had rented out the house and our tenant had a one-year lease through September. So Penny and I decided, okay, we'd finish off the basement ourselves and move into the in-law in May. If we hadn't given ourselves the option of creating an in-law, we would never have been able to finish in time."

Once they'd committed to creating an in-law unit, its layout flowed easily (see the floor plan above). Placing the bathroom toward the back of the house and away from the door made sense for several reasons:

- a bathroom is easier to heat if it's not on an exterior wall
- windows are less important to a bathroom than to living and dining areas
- plumbing stacks and pipes were already routed through the back of the building
- because the crawlspace under the house decreased dramatically toward the hill behind the house, the back of the unit was the best place for a room whose ceiling could be a little lower without sacrificing comfort

Tiling usually stops at the opening of a shower, but Tuer decided to have fun and return (wrap) tile around the opening and continue it onto the outside walls. Curiously enough, the expanse of tiles makes the tiny (4½ ft. x 5 ft.) bathroom feel larger.

THE APPEAL OF NICE FINISH DETAILS—custom cabinets, wood floors, quality windows, a tiled bath—can help counteract the small space of an in-law unit. And the nicer it is, the choosier you can be about whom you rent to.

The bathroom makes the most of what little floor space was available. With its back wall snug against the hill, the bathroom ekes out a 7 ft.-6 in. ceiling, and there's just enough room for a stacked washer-dryer. Three steps go down 18 in. into the living area, whose ceiling is a full 8 ft. With the bathroom tucked into the eastern corner of the back wall, it was logical to place the kitchen in the other corner so that it could enjoy a tiny window high on the western wall and accommodate a kitchen island that doubled as an eating area. It's a tight fit but it works (see the photos on the facing page). The back counter butts against bedrock. Consequently, it is only 18 in. wide (rather than a standard 24 in.) and there are no cabinets below it—just panels that hide the rock. Locating the kitchen and eating area near the front door make the most of natural ventilation and gentle breezes during the summer.

The area remaining after the kitchen and bath were located had to serve as both living and sleeping areas—with only 340 sq. ft. in the entire unit, there wasn't room for a separate bedroom. The solution was to include a fold-up Murphy bed, and it was obvious where it would go—on the last unused section of the wall between the kitchen and the bathroom (see the photos on pp. 116–117). Behind the bed is a bearing wall and bedrock, while in front of it, lovely long views out the windows.

Except for laminate countertops, the kitchen materials are natural: recycled fir cabinets and paneling, local maple floors, and a butcher block eating counter. Though the refrigerator is only ¾ size, it sits on a 12-in.-high platform that raises it to the same height as a full-size model. It's a bit of a visual trick: If the top is at a familiar height, the smaller version seems less like a dinky fridge.

BELOW: The raised eating counter is a hunk of butcher block cantilevered off a structural post. To make the most of magnificent views, the architect specified a thin mullion between two fixed double-pane windows, with awning windows below for ventilation.

The living-sleeping area feels spacious because of abundant natural light, long views, clean sight lines, and light-colored reflective surfaces such as birch plywood wall panels and maple flooring. The underside of the Murphy bed is just visible at right.

THE FLOOR CAN BE AN IMPORTANT SOURCE of reflected light in a basement in-law. If you're considering wood floors, a highly finished, light-colored wood such as maple is a good choice. Light-colored materials also make a space feel larger.

THE GOLDEN RULE OF RENTING

The materials used throughout the in-law balance empathy, good taste, and a green sensibility. When they had first moved out west, the Tuers lived in an in-law in Whistler, B. C., so they knew what it was like to live downstairs in somebody else's house. So they decided to finish their in-law "really nice . . . in a manner that we would want to live in."

For the floors in the kitchen and the living area, the Tuers chose ¾-in. Canadian maple, a local product that was readily available and quick to install because it came prefinished. They wanted maple for its durability and lighter color, which bounces the light around a lot more, and so makes the rooms bright even on an overcast day. For the bathroom floor and its companion landing, they chose Douglas fir tongue-and-groove decking left over from the roof construction. Sanded down, the fir was nice enough for flooring and being somewhat rustic it coexisted nicely with the textured bathroom tile.

PUTTING PASSIVE DESIGN TO WORK

Passive solar design, which employs natural forces to conserve resources and increase comfort, was a big part of the Tuers' project. The main house is very much a passive solar house with generous south- and east-facing glass and concrete floors for thermal mass. But the in-law suite also has many passive features.

The apartment's oversize window to the east allows the winter morning sun to enter and heat the interior, and large south-facing windows help fill the open areas with natural light. During the summer, the deck above doubles as a solar shade to limit the amount of direct sun. Operable windows on the south and east walls cross-ventilate and cool the space in the summer. The back wall of the in-law abuts bedrock, so the earth's year-round temperature of 55°F tends to cool the house in the summer and moderate extreme cold spells in the winter. Combined with a super-insulated floor, that makes the in-law cheap to heat. □

The head of the bed fits into a recess that creates intimacy in the open space. Steps up to the raised bathroom level, in turn, create an *en–suite* that's close to but distinct from the sleeping area. A stacked washer-dryer is hidden by the fabric, at right.

CHAPTER 6

garage conversions

CONVERTING A GARAGE DIRECTLY INTO AN IN-LAW can be one of the most affordable ways to gain extra living space. If four walls are already in place, you'll save a chunk of money on materials. The framing is accessible, and having a driveway close by makes carting off debris and hauling supplies a snap. Garage in-laws are popular because they're often easy to provide with good natural light and ventilation. They tend to be private, too, offering an ideal space for almost any tenant from relative to renter.

If the new in-law will be inside a garage, be sure to check zoning regulations early on. You may have to add parking spaces to replace the ones you turn into living space. And if the new suite will sit above a garage, consult an engineer and keep an eye on building codes because they include specific requirements designed to maintain your safety and health.

turning a box into a beauty

T here was nothing wrong with the Finches' old garage except that it was too far from the house to park in and was, well, just a 20-ft. by 28-ft. box. So, after extensively remodeling their home, landscaping the grounds, and adding a parking apron near the main house, the Finches naturally trained their sights on the unloved box in the backyard.

BELOW: To make the cottage more light-filled and less boxy, the architect added a monitor to the roof and a modest shed-roofed bump-out that overlooks the yard.

RIGHT: Before the garage (at right), was reborn as a guest cottage, part of a neighboring lot was added to the property. The building whose roof is just visible at left was razed and the concrete pad removed.

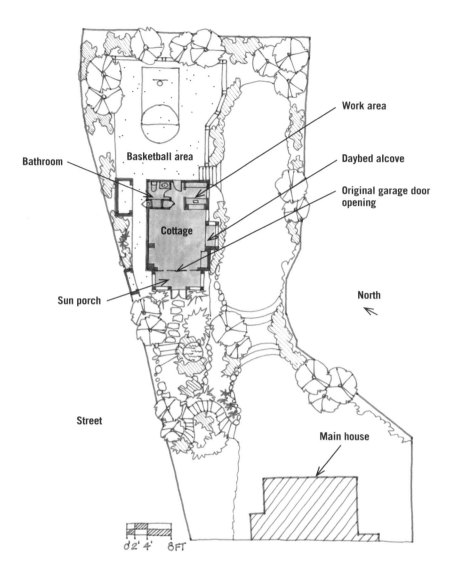

Work area

Daybed alcove

Original garage door opening

Basketball area

Bathroom

Cottage

North

Sun porch

Street

Main house

0 2' 4' 8FT

The family's wish list for a garage redo was an architect's dream, which is to say, pretty much a blank slate. The Finches' main requirements for the guest cottage were that it be light, airy, easy to maintain, and comfortable enough for a long stay. Also, when guests weren't in the cottage, it would be great if the space could be used as a family room or workout room. Everyone in the family was a decent basketball player and there was a level area behind the garage, so space for a hoop was added to the agenda.

PUSHING OUT AND UP

Architect Arleta Chang's first response to the family's requests was to push out. She began by bumping out a 6-ft. by 16-ft. sun porch to the west to get afternoon sun and create an interesting entrance (see the photo above). That end of the garage was already framed for a 16-ft.-wide garage door so the sun porch could be easily added to the structure. A street ran along the north side

of the garage, so the original builder had not put any windows there. That would make sense to preserve privacy in the cottage, so Chang left that side of the building alone. The logical place to add windows and gain light, therefore, was on the south side, which overlooked the yard. Midway along the wall, Chang added a daybed alcove (see the sidebar on p. 122) with large double-hung windows topped with fixed transom windows. But she wasn't quite done.

Casting about for some way to tie the cottage to the 1910 Arts and Crafts house and get more natural light into the interior of the cottage, she opted for a *monitor* (a lengthwise cupola that runs along the ridge of the building and is open to the interior; see the sidebar on p. 123). Particularly popular on barns in the nineteenth century, a monitor added an old-fashioned appearance and delivered soft indirect light throughout the cottage. Once the windows were hooked to a remote control device that made it easy to open and close them, the monitor also became an important source of cross-ventilation. The box was no longer a box.

The sun porch, which looks somewhat like a trellis that got roofed, provides a nice transition from outside to inside. An end view of the monitor is visible atop the roof.

ROOM FOR ONE

A daybed alcove can create intimacy and interest in what would otherwise be a large open room. People naturally gravitate toward the walls or corners of a big room because they seem cozy and safe. That's why, in a partially filled restaurant, the tables in the middle are often empty. As a bonus, there's usually ample room for storage under a daybed.

A daybed alcove (with storage drawers below) is a great place to nap or read a book.

The roof monitor and exposed rafters give the cottage a playful, rather barnlike feel. The support beams and rafters divide the ceiling into structural bays, which is more interesting than a vast expanse of drywall; likewise, the board-and-batten wainscot jazzes up the walls.

GARAGE SLABS OFTEN SLOPE, either toward an interior drain or toward garage door openings, the better to shed water that gets in. Though a topping slab of concrete can level such slopes, framed floors call for a different approach: You'll have to shim or taper-cut subfloor framing. For an example of this method, see p. 29.

Refining the floor plan was largely a matter of balancing related activity areas. A bathroom and a work area are located on the east end of the cottage, close to the basketball court. Roughly in the middle of the cottage, Chang placed a closed storage area across from the niche that contains a Murphy bed and built-in bookcases (see the top photo on p. 124).

A SLAB FOR ALL SEASONS

As plain as the old garage was, it was solidly constructed, particularly its foundation and slab. Unlike many older concrete floors without steel reinforcement, this slab showed only minor surface cracks. And because an extensive drainage system had been installed around the garage perimeter when the property was landscaped, surface moisture was not a concern.

Adding radiant heat called for installing flexible tubing in a 4-in. reinforced concrete topping slab poured over the old floor. The topping slab leveled out irregularities and slopes in the old floor, and was a perfect substrate for the slate finished floor that followed. As it turns out, the radiant heating has been used only on the coldest days, thanks to the passive solar heat gain from the south-facing windows. Radiant heat is an especially appropriate way to heat large rooms, where the heated air

The curved brackets above the work area are a faint echo of their sun porch cousins. Otherwise, all molding is stock San Francisco Victoriana, with a crown molding fashioned from flat trim set at a 45° angle rather than a more traditional (and more formal) ogee profile.

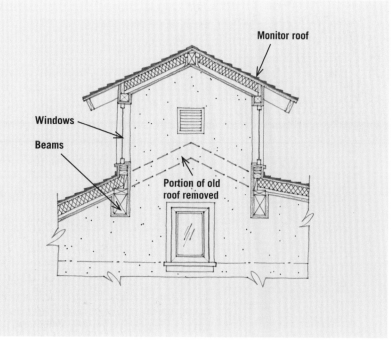

MAKING A MONITOR

A monitor is a long and narrow area of raised roof with windows on each side. There are various ways to frame one, but in this case the vertical walls of the monitor were supported by glulam beams. The beams also support the rafter-ends of the old roof, which were severed to create the rough opening for the monitor.

Monitor roof

Windows

Beams

Portion of old roof removed

Inside, the porch is delineated by a pair of curved brackets, which are visually more graceful than, say, stumpy columns. The brackets and built-in bookcase create a sense of enclosure and privacy for the Murphy bed.

of a forced-air system would quickly rise and dissipate. The heated mass of a radiant floor gives off warmth more slowly and evenly and is much less likely to create drafts. A bonus: no heating registers or convectors will complicate the placement of furniture.

The green slate floor was a good choice. Despite frequent use of the cottage since it was finished, the slate shows few signs of wear. And it fits the character of the place, whatever that is at the moment—garden shed, party room, sports pavilion, music studio, or refuge for a weary traveler. □

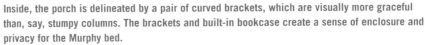

The bathroom is elegant but spare, equally suited for visiting parents or basketball players making a quick pit stop between pickup games. A skylight keeps the bathroom from feeling claustrophobic while preserving privacy from traffic on the street.

billy's place

When his wife of more than 50 years passed away, Billy Bye was lost. "He was rattling around in his townhouse in Minneapolis alone," his daughter-in-law Heidi recalled. "So my husband Jim and I said, 'Why don't you live with us? We'll fix up the in-law over the garage for you.' " Without missing a beat, Billy agreed.

NEW LIFE FOR AN OLD IN-LAW

Heidi and Jim Bye were almost done remodeling their house, so their designer and builder were available to start work immediately on the garage project. Someone had lived over the garage years before, but the space was in rough shape. It had never been insulated, had only plywood floors and rudimentary plumbing, and the frames and sash of most of the windows were rotted. Curiously, though, its basic floor plan was promising: two dormers created an alcove large enough for a kitchen on one side and a bed nook on the other (see the floor plan on p. 126).

Billy's in-law over the garage, near Lake Minnetonka. The bank of large windows in the gable end illuminates the living room and office nook.

While Heidi and designer Ron Brenner refined the layout and chose materials and appliances, builder Mike Herman reframed the structure and installed new electrical, plumbing, heating, and central air-conditioning. That done, he was ready to insulate all around the apartment, including its floor. Each time the garage doors opened during winter, a huge amount of heat escaped from the garage below. Also, insulation would soundproof the floor to a degree from engine noise.

Because the old roof lacked eave and ridge vents and adding them would have meant rebuilding the roof, Herman opted for a hot roof system (sometimes called an unvented roof). In this system, closed-cell foam insulation (usually, polyurethane) is sprayed on the underside of the roof, filling rafter bays. In addition to insulating, the foam also seals air leaks and prevents moisture from condensing on the underside of the roof and rotting the framing and sheathing—a big problem in harsh Minnesota winters. In this case, a heating-cooling unit located in the garage conditions the air within the insulated shell.

A NEW START FOR BILLY

Once the drywall was up, the renovation proceeded quickly, with Billy stopping by from time to time to cheer on the crews. At one end of his new home were gleaming wood floors, a full bathroom, and a new fireplace mantel and tile surround. At the other end, a carpeted area doubles as a living room and home office. The U-shaped kitchen has plenty of counter and cabinet space, every

SISTER POWER

When creating an in-law apartment under a gable roof—whether over a garage or in an attic—you may find rafters that sag, twist, or whose edges simply don't line up. Whatever the situation, you must first create a flat plane on each ceiling surface before installing drywall. Otherwise the finish ceiling will look wavy and uneven or, worse, seams may split and sheets pull free.

Sistering refers to nailing or bolting new rafters, joists, or studs to existing ones to improve their ability to bear loads or to create a flat plane to attach sheet materials to. On the Bye project, the contractor sistered new rafters to the old ones. As he added each new rafter, he aligned its underside to taut strings running across the top and bottom of each rafter group.

Floor Plan

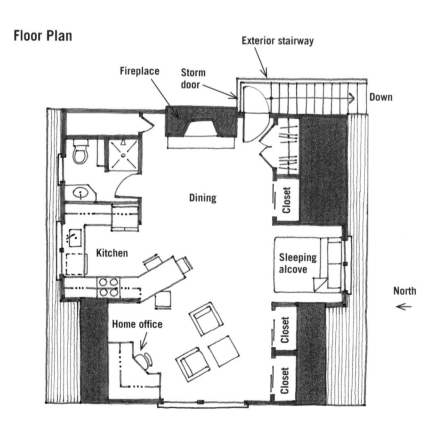

CREATING A WEALTH OF STORAGE SPACES

Adding interior knee walls is a great way to gain storage because it makes use of otherwise unusable floor space under sloping roofs. The farther you bring the knee wall into the room, the higher your storage area will be (but the more floor space you'll lose). To avoid cold areas and moisture problems caused by condensation, fully insulate the storage area to isolate it from cold weather.

ABOVE: Extensive built-in cabinets around the perimeter of the apartment help make it spacious and uncluttered.

RIGHT: An existing dormer was the perfect size for a bed nook. Because there was no room for nightstands, built-in shelves do the job.

In the other corner of the living area, a home office tucks under the sloping ceiling.

One end of the suite is a happy hodgepodge of cabinets, cutouts, and complex angles. The fireplace provides a warm welcome; the door to the stairway is at right.

A dining peninsula runs off one leg of a U-shaped kitchen. The table is set at an angle so it doesn't impede access to the living area and bed nook.

appliance a fellow could want, and an eating peninsula that extends off one side of the U. Brenner set the table at an angle so that it wouldn't crowd the bed nook (see the right photo above). And around the perimeter of the in-law there's plenty of storage. Built-in closets and drawers, clad in beadboard, tuck under the space beneath the sloping ceilings.

Billy loved his new place and many mornings he came down to the house to have coffee with Heidi. One morning, after he had been there about six months, he informed her that he was ready to leave his sadness behind and start dating, whereupon he pulled out a list of about 25 eligible women, many of whom he had known since grade school. After dating three women on the list, Billy was introduced to one who wasn't, and it was love at first sight.

After a few dates, Billy brought Sally back to his place over the garage. Music was playing and candles were lit. Without really moving from the spot where they stood, Billy gave Sally a tour. He said, "Well, here's my kitchen, and this is my bedroom and there's my family room and that's my office." Then they turned back toward the fireplace, which had a fire blazing in it. Taking Sally in his arms, Billy said, "And this is my dance floor."

Within the year, they were married. □

the 15-second commute

Little girls are among the immutable forces of nature. So when it became a question of whether Ed Scheuer would move his office out of the house or his three daughters would be as still as church mice when clients called, the answer was never much in doubt. Fortunately, there was a 400-sq.-ft. garage in the backyard that wasn't doing much, and the half that Ed wouldn't need as an office would be a great place for Gram and Grandpa to stay when they visited from England.

The old flat-roofed garage was sound, so converting it to an in-law was largely a matter of framing openings for window walls on two sides and new French doors facing the backyard.

By exactly matching the doors, windows, heavy trim, and shingle siding of the main house (at left), the in-law now looks more like a garden building than a garage.

A HELPFUL CONSTRAINT

The garage was in decent shape for a mid-'70s structure—a little water damage here and there, a sagging beam or two, and the general mustiness of a dark, unheated space. When Ed and Mary Ann met with architect Robin Pennell to discuss the conversion, they learned of one more shortcoming. The south and west walls of the garage were right on the property line; to satisfy local fire codes, they couldn't add any windows to those walls. The reasoning, in brief, was that windows would allow a fire in the garage to spread too easily to adjoining properties. Curiously, that constraint simplified their design decision making.

If they couldn't have windows south and west, Pennell suggested, they should load up on the north and east sides, creating window walls that looked toward the house and into the backyard. Needing natural light, Ed's office would occupy the north part of the space, while the guest bedroom would take the south part. A freestanding bookshelf unit would divide the two areas (see the top photo on the facing page). A small bathroom could then fit nicely into the northwest corner, where it could have a small north-facing window. With the addition of two skylights to balance the natural light and a post to support a tired 4x12 beam, the layout was decided. A remaining sliver of the garage on the southeast corner would house bikes, tools, and a natural gas on-demand water heater.

Floor Plan

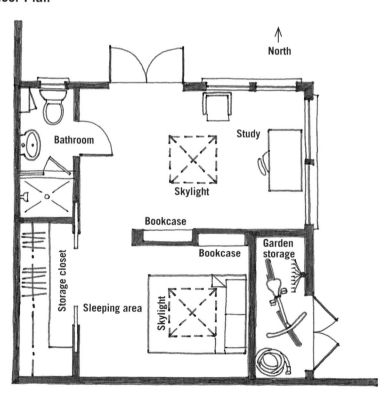

North

Bathroom

Study

Skylight

Bookcase

Bookcase

Garden storage

Storage closet

Sleeping area

Skylight

A Douglas fir "yin and yang" bookcase separates the bedroom from the office so that each side has an expanse of clear paneling and some shelves.

This tiny (4 ft. by 6½ ft.) bathroom accommodates three fixtures without feeling cramped. Two details help make this possible: a wall-hung cabinet frees up floor space and the lavatory stand comes out from the wall only 10 in.

PITCH, PIPES, AND FALL

Adding a bathroom to a garage often means cutting into a concrete slab, one of the most disagreeable tasks in renovation. If you can position the DWV (drain-waste-vent) pipes close to an exterior wall, as the Scheuers were able to do, you won't have to cut through as much concrete and you'll spare yourself a lot of grief. Except for a small section of slab and sidewalk that their drainpipe had to cross, excavation for the pipe was in dirt, not concrete. The pipe continued through the backyard until it connected to the house's main drain.

Drainpipes must maintain a minimum downward pitch of ⅛ in. per ft. so wastes and water can flow freely; this amount of "fall" is critical. Otherwise, you must use a sewage ejection pump to move wastes along. The old floor in the Scheuers' garage was somewhat low but because they chose to install radiant heating, which requires a 4-in.-thick topping slab, they gained just enough elevation for wastes to flow freely.

The window walls facing north and east are comprised of smaller transom windows that swing out to provide cross-ventilation, with casements below that are usually kept closed. The radiant concrete floor was acid-etched for a deeper, more complex color.

MODERATION IN ALL THINGS

Working within the existing footprint and leaving the garage roof intact kept costs down, though there were second thoughts about the roof. The issue was heat buildup. The San Francisco Bay Area's moderate climate never gets terribly cold in the winter but a dark flat roof can soak up a lot of heat in the summer. The garage's 2x4 rafters didn't provide much depth for insulation, and tearing apart a good roof to add larger rafters seemed wasteful. There was an even more compelling reason for leaving the roof alone, though: the garage's 10-ft. height was the maximum allowed by city codes.

The solution was threefold. Spraying expanding foam insulation between the rafters provided a greater R-value than, say, fiberglass batts. Adding a row of awning windows along the top of Ed's window walls (see the photo below) provided cross-ventilation and a place for hot air to escape. The last piece of the puzzle was the radiant floor system. During the cooler months, it provides heat that is so even that Ed can work in his socks. But because the concrete floor gets no direct sunlight, it remains cool in the summer and thus moderates the room's temperature even on the hottest days.

Except for occasional gymnastic displays in the backyard, the office has few distractions. Notes Ed, "It's perfect: I've got a 15-second commute. My office is so close that I can work any time—of course, that's the downside, too." □

WHEN CHOOSING WINDOWS, consider each room's use. In a home office, for example, avoid window schemes that place visually heavy elements in the sight line of someone sitting. In Ed's office, the horizontal mullion separating upper and lower windows is well above his seated eye level.

a winter's tale

S ometimes life is a balancing act. The confines of an old house must address the needs of a new family. The demands of a long winter challenge the desire for warmth and comfort. And the wishes of two strong, well-meaning people who see things just a bit differently somehow have to be reconciled.

When Cheryl and Tom first saw the stately Victorian above Michigan's Huron River, they were of one mind: They wanted it. After exploring inside the 1869 brick building and strolling its manicured lawns, they tromped down a steep embankment choked with berry bushes and brambles, toward the river. At the bottom of the hill, Tom looked back up at the house and said, "If I were an eight-year-old kid, this is where I would want to grow up."

Overall, it was a wonderful place with a lot of personality. Shortly after buying it, the couple began a series of thoughtful remodels—a new kitchen, plumbing and wiring upgrades, a second upstairs bathroom—that respected the house's original style. But as the years rolled by and their family grew, it became increasingly obvious that some parts of the house just weren't working very well.

The house, before. A 1920s renovation added a *porte cochère* with a shed roof to the east face of the house. Unfortunately, it was not wide enough for modern cars.

The new garage houses an in-law suite above. To visually tie the new structure to the main house, the architect repeated Italianate elements such as arched doors and windows, and a modest balcony.

The south face of the house better shows the new addition's scale. From left to right, sunroom, main house, breezeway, and new garage in-law.

THREE PRESSING ISSUES

For starters, there was no place for visitors to stay. The house looked big because it was tall, but it was actually very narrow. By the time Cheryl and Tom had carved out a master bedroom, added a second bathroom, and had three daughters, the four bedrooms were all occupied.

There was also an odd structure on the east face of the house, a *porte cochere* added sometime in the 1920s. Though perfectly sized for a Ford Model A, it was so narrow that full-size modern cars barely fit. It was also so dark under the porte cochere that visitors coming up the drive often couldn't see the entrance under it. Consequently, guests wandered around to the back of the house and thus entered directly into the living room, wet coats, dripping umbrellas, muddy boots and all.

Perhaps the most pressing and intractable problem, however, was the lack of a garage. During the long Michigan winters, snow near the house would be driven over, packed down, and turned into sheet ice. Once the kids started coming, Cheryl lobbied for a garage that was close to the house, clean, and dry. Tom, on the other hand, wanted a detached garage that wouldn't block

Floor Plan

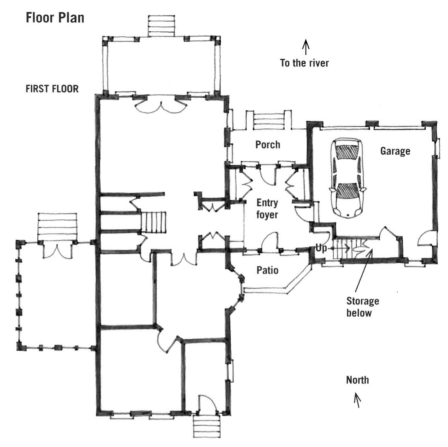

FIRST FLOOR

To the river

Porch

Garage

Entry
foyer

Up

Patio

Storage
below

North

SECOND FLOOR

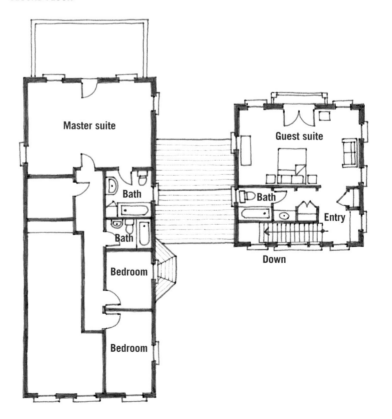

Master suite

Guest suite

Bath

Bath

Bath

Entry

Bedroom

Down

Bedroom

In the suite's bedroom, French doors open onto a small balcony and long views toward the river.

At the top of the stairs from the breezeway to the in-law suite, a built-in bench welcomes visitors.

The suite's bathroom also incorporates Victorian touches such as a pedestal sink, an inset band of colored tiles, and an arched window.

any house windows. In fact, he thought a detached garage 50 ft. or 100 ft. away from the house would look more as if an old barn had been converted—more 1800s, in other words. He held on to this manly love of tromping through the snow for some time. So every six months they'd revisit the issue, lay out their cases, and realize that nobody's mind had changed.

TWO ROADS NOT TAKEN . . . AND ONE THAT WAS

As Cheryl and Tom discussed their needs, they became aware that an in-law suite could be a part of any solution. So they considered several configurations with an in-law.

A bump-out addition seemed plausible at first. But unlike many old houses that are dark and spooky, their Victorian had a lot of light thanks to large windows (7 ft. or 8 ft. tall and 3 ft. wide) throughout. Any place they grafted on a bump-out would significantly impact the amount of light coming into that room. No good.

A detached garage with an in-law unit upstairs would solve the problem of where to put visiting relatives. Despite her reservations about safety and convenience, Cheryl did think a detached unit could be visually appealing. So

Light-filled and spacious, the breezeway is a favorite of the family.
It's a great place for reading on a dark day, tumbling on the carpet, or
practicing your whirling.

The breezeway doubles as a mudroom, with
plenty of built-in storage.

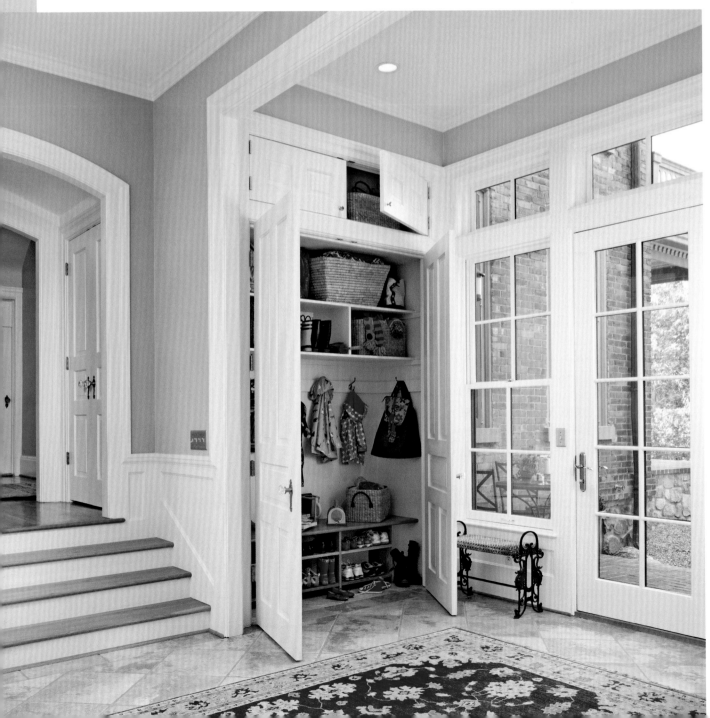

MAKING GARAGE UNITS SAFE

When there's a living space above a garage, getting the details right is important for health and safety. Your local building authority has the final say, but the following tips can help make your unit a safer, more pleasant place to be:

- Install fire-resistant (Type X) drywall on garage walls and ceilings. The thicker the panel, the higher its fire rating; a thickness of ⅝ in. is often specified. On walls and ceilings between a garage and living space, fire codes may require two layers of Type X drywall.

- Spray insulation is a good choice to insulate the floors of in-law units over garages. It seals cracks and effectively deadens the transmission of sound.

- Install a motion-sensor exhaust system to clear the garage of noxious fumes. Typically an exhaust fan starts when a car pulls in or out, and runs until a timer switch shuts it off.

throughout the fall, she and Tom tried parking by the barn, about 100 ft. east of the house. But as soon as bad weather blew in, nine out of ten times they would park next to the house. "Why build a garage you use only on nice days?" wondered Cheryl.

Fortunately, Tom found the answer to their dilemma while driving along a road in southern Illinois. In a little town near the Mississippi River, he noticed a converted barn-garage attached—by a breezeway—to an old farmhouse. Largely glass, the breezeway didn't cut off light where it joined the house, didn't make the house look clunky, and provided a covered passageway to the garage in bad weather. Not long after, Tom and Cheryl sat down with architect Michael Klement to see if this solution might work for them.

Klement showed them a number of designs for a garage with an in-law suite above and a one-story breezeway connecting the garage to the main house. Together, they searched for the best balance of scale (in relation to the main house) and usable space, then added details that echoed Italianate elements of the main house. Ultimately, the couple chose a two-car garage design with a one-bedroom in-law above. The final piece of the puzzle was figuring out where to place it. For a variety of reasons, the logical spot to connect a breezeway was at the *porte cochère*, which they happily removed.

A HARDWORKING BREEZEWAY

Now the house works, and the breezeway is a big part of that success. Cheryl has a dry indoor place to unload the car and the kids, and even Tom has begun to warm to the space. Visitors stopping by on a stormy night have a grand mudroom in which to store their gear. On a sunny day, the breezeway is Tom's favorite place to sit and read. And grandma and grandpa can stay as long as they like without disturbing anybody's routine, quite content in their in-law retreat, framed by French doors that open onto a balcony facing north, toward the river. □

CHAPTER 7

stand-alone
in-laws

IF YOU HAVE A LARGE ENOUGH PROPERTY,
building a stand-alone in-law unit will give you
the most design options, the greatest degree of
privacy, and, ultimately, the greatest selection of
tenants. Almost everyone wants to live in a cozy
cottage surrounded by greenery. Who knows?
You may decide to live there yourself one day.

A building designed from scratch can be
tailored to the needs of the person who will
live in it—whether the barrier-free needs of a
person using a wheelchair or walker, or a young
adult who needs a multifunctional space that
can double as a home office or a workshop. But
don't stop there. Think about what you'd like
to be doing 10 or 20 years from now and make
room for that, too, in the design of your new
in-law cottage.

rethinking what you really need

D esigners Tolya and Otto Stonorov didn't set out to live permanently in 400 sq. ft. But the tiny two-story barn stood empty on their new property and they figured they could live in it while they renovated the main house. Besides, the barn was, well, sort of cute. Later on, once they moved into the main house, it could serve as an in-law for guests or a studio.

A 100-year-old barn was reborn as a rustic urban retreat, thanks to double doors that open onto a landscaped patio, oversized window casing that doubles as an outdoor window seat, and a rain-screen exterior of rough-sawn spruce strips.

YOU SHOULD ALWAYS HAVE A HOUSE PROFESSIONALLY INSPECTED before buying it, but you can learn a lot even before spending money for a formal inspection. To detect rot around the base of a building, use a penknife or flat-blade screwdriver gently to probe its mudsills, sheathing, and siding. If the point sinks in to a depth of ½ in. or more, rot is probable but depending on the extent of the problem, it might not be a deal-breaker.

SIMPLIFYING DESIGN CHOICES

Once they began gutting the barn, the Stonorovs wondered what had been holding it up. Ivy was growing through the walls, its redwood foundation was gone, and much of its wall framing was riddled with rot and insect holes. Wasting no time, they jacked up the barn and supported its upper story with shoring. After pouring a concrete foundation and floor slab, they framed the first floor. The project took on a new urgency when, two months into it, Tolya learned she was pregnant. Their son Niko was born three months after the barn was finished.

Floor Plan

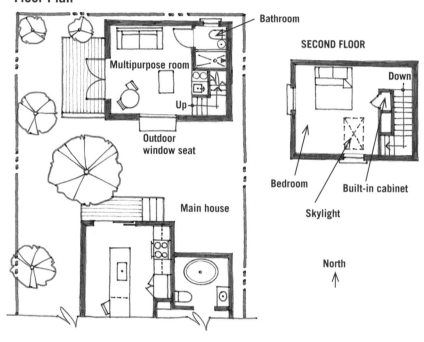

The large window of the in-law (see the photo on p. 141) looks across a pleasant courtyard into the open-air kitchen of the main house, right.

LEFT: Built-ins help keep the upstairs calm and collected, and shield the stairs from view.

RIGHT: The bedroom is composed and peaceful, with almost every window looking out onto greenery. In the corner is a crib Tolya and Otto made for Niko.

As it turned out, the barn's location in the northeast corner of a long narrow lot simplified the Stonorov's design choices. The two sides of the building that sat on property lines couldn't be changed, so the barn's new entrance would face west, toward the path from the street. This would also give the unit a modicum of privacy if it ever became a rental. On the remaining wall, facing the main house, there's a combination of windows surrounded by oversized Douglas fir "casing" that serves as a window seat. That seat is supported in part by an angle bar bolted to the wall framing. The house and in-law create a courtyard of sorts so the window box is a good place to relax and watch Niko play or to chat with whoever's making dinner in the main house.

Their design choices were further circumscribed by the building's 12-ft. x 16-ft. footprint. There was room for one multipurpose area downstairs (see the photo on p. 144) and a bedroom-nursery upstairs (see the photos above). The bathroom went into the northeast corner, the most private spot on the first floor, while a tiny kitchenette was built into the stairwell wall. In fact, built-ins were an essential part of optimizing space and controlling clutter—that, and making do with less.

HAVING LESS AND LOVING IT, MOSTLY

The kitchenette is a study in minimalism, though from time to time Tolya uses it to whip up a meal for six. Its heart is a two-burner glass cooktop sitting on a concrete counter, flanked by a 6-in.-wide sink that, Tolya freely admits, is ridiculously small. To supplement the dearth of counter space, they rely on a stainless-steel kitchen island found online at a restaurant supplier. It holds

The first floor is a living-dining-cooking room with colorful etched-concrete floors. Because the couple has a small child, the room has no sharp corners. At left, the door to the bathroom.

most of their appliances—notably their coffee grinder and their espresso maker—and in a pinch you can put a hot pan on the island without harm. Beneath the concrete counter is an apartment-size refrigerator. Nobody would recommend a kitchenette this small as a permanent arrangement, but in this case it worked because:

- They knew it was temporary.
- They were so busy rearing a child and renovating the main house that they rarely had time to cook complicated meals.
- Double doors facing west expanded their living space by encouraging grilling and eating outside.
- Fresh produce was available year-round in their Oakland, California, neighborhood, so they shopped often, ate fresh, and had less food to store. In short, they made use of their community's resources.

Tolya and Otto are convinced that the cozy confines of Niko's bedroom and his play area—and even the stairs—helped him master his world at an earlier age. He's a very confident little guy. And whenever it got too frenetic inside the little house, that was a great time to go for a walk and see what was going on in the world beyond the fence. □

a place for singing

By the time Nancy Kimura's mother, Stella, began calling in the middle of the night, wondering why the bus to the senior center was late, it was pretty clear that she could no longer live alone in her home of more than 50 years. But where would she go?

Stella Kimura is a proud woman who had become even more independent after her husband's death, so putting her in an assisted living facility felt like "a death knell" to Nancy and her husband, Marc. They considered moving into Stella's house, but it would have offered little privacy. And moving during their son's final year in high school was just too disruptive. So they began thinking about adding an in-law to their property.

An L-shaped floor plan with a patio has a lot going for it: abundant natural light and ventilation, a pleasant place to take meals or relax when the weather is nice —and plenty of privacy. The house and trellis surround the patio on three sides.

ADDING AN IN-LAW COTTAGE

Because their backyard is small, Nancy and Marc's first inclination was to add several rooms to their house as a bump-out. However, one manifestation of Alzheimer's disease is a need to repeat phrases. Stella would sing incessantly or count to three for hours on end, so it became apparent that physical separation was an essential part of any workable solution. Thus, they settled on a cottage in the backyard. "Mother is sweet," Nancy mused, "but the racket she made would have driven us crazy."

About the time they decided to build a cottage, Nancy and Marc noticed a tiny writer's studio featured in a magazine and contacted its architect, Anne Phillips. Anne encouraged them to make a list of things their in-law cottage had to do, so they got right on it:

- It has to feel like a little house, with a kitchen. Mother doesn't cook any more, but if she becomes bed-ridden somebody could come in and cook for her.
- It must be light and airy.
- She must be safe as well as *feel* safe moving around indoors.
- It must be easy to keep an eye on her, because sometimes she wanders off.
- They should be able to see into the cottage from the main house.

Phillips brought a deep understanding of universal design (see p. 212) to the project. To minimize falls, she designed everything on one level. To accommodate Stella's possible future use of a walker, a wheelchair, or a hospital bed, she made door openings and passageways at least 3 ft. wide. The bathroom is simple and accessible, with a sturdy grab rail by the tub.

Floor Plan

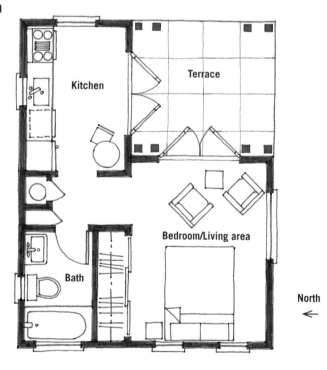

Kitchen

Terrace

Bedroom/Living area

Bath

North
←

OLDER PEOPLE
APPRECIATE
the lack of steps
going from indoors
to outdoors, but
completely flat and
level surfaces aren't
ideal. Place patios at
least 2 to 3 in. below
the level of interior
floors. Otherwise,
water collecting on
the patio could run
inside the house and
cause water damage.
In addition, slope
patios gently away
from the building at
a rate of $1/16$ in. to
$1/8$ in. per lineal
foot so they'll drain
properly.

Floor surfaces are concrete throughout, scored with a rectangular pattern to minimize cracking and make the slab a bit more interesting to look at.

To reduce the confusion that frequently overwhelms people with dementia, Phillips all but eliminated hallways and interior doors. Only the bathroom has a door and the only hallway is a small area where it's possible to look into all three rooms—bedroom, bathroom, kitchen—at the same time. "People with Alzheimer's can get lost in their own homes," Phillips explained. "So you have to reduce the number of choices they must make to get around. Any choice that confuses them can become an obstacle."

WORKING WITH ZONING REGULATIONS

Planning departments often use a formula, based upon the percentage of a lot that will be covered by buildings, to determine the maximum footprint of a secondary dwelling. In this case, the cottage could be no larger than 340 sq. ft. of enclosed space. Fortunately, patios and courtyards are not usually included when calculating enclosed space. So Phillips was able to design an L-shaped plan whose sides open onto a patio, without exceeding the size limits. For anyone with a small lot, a layout like that makes plenty of sense. In warmer months, the patio becomes an outdoor room, and any time of year all the glass that faces it lets in a lot of light.

An L-shaped floor plan is also a good design for an urban dwelling if its largest windows—in this case, sliding glass doors in the kitchen and bedroom—face into the patio and yard rather than looking out into neighboring properties. The Kimura cottage feels private and respects the privacy of houses on either side. Along the back wall of the cottage, which is quite close to the property line, the windows are small and placed high up for the same reason. The large glass doors into the bedroom also allow Nancy to keep an eye on her mother from the main house.

Nancy and Stella Kimura enjoy the patio, which, in nice weather, extends the indoor space.

Oversized elements can make small homes feel commodious. Here, high ceilings and a soaring arched window create an expansive sense of space. On a bright day, concrete floors radiate warmth long after the sun is down.

Be sure to make room for the things you love. In the foreground, a painting Mrs. Kimura painted in her '90s; in the far corner, a sketch of Mt. Fuji made when she was a high school student.

LIGHT AND AIRY

Thanks to the sliding doors and windows on every wall, the cottage is blessed with plenty of natural ventilation. The sliding doors are 8 ft. tall (standard height is 6 ft. 8 in.), which is unusually large for such a small house, but they make the place feel bigger. As long as there's any daylight left, you can see into the furthest reaches of any cabinet or closet without turning on a light.

The crown jewel of the design and the source of much of that light is the south wall of the bedroom, which rises to a 12-ft.-high ridge and frames a dramatic arched window (see the left photo above). The window floods the room with sunlight and warms up the concrete floors so effectively that the cottage heating bills are modest year-round. A younger person would probably hang curtains to block some of that solar gain but old people like it hot. Thus, on most days when Nancy goes out to the cottage to check on her mother, she finds her rocking in front of the window, watching the Japanese cable station, doing her art work, and, often as not, singing. □

lisa's baby

Given the importance of universal design, a small army of architects, engineers, and social scientists have no doubt sliced, diced, and digested the data used to create buildings and environments that work for people of all ages. Lisa Lum's design method was somewhat simpler, but no less insightful: If she could walk easily through a doorway with a baby on her hip, it was probably also wide enough for a grandparent using a walker.

Though it uses many of the same elements as the main house—such as French doors, a muted color palette, similar roof pitches, and a trellis—this in-law cottage is not simply a small version of the house.

ON BEING YOUR OWN GENERAL CONTRACTOR

General contractors must master a number of skills, including estimating and scheduling, pulling permits, ordering materials, managing crewmembers and subs, troubleshooting plans, and so on. It's a complex job and GCs work hard; so will you. However, if you want to try it:

Start small. In Lisa Lum's case, she had overseen the renovation of her home and had managed a remodel for her parents before attempting this ambitious project.

Learn the lingo and the sequence of construction. If possible, first hire a contractor for another project and learn all you can from him or her. Become a student of the trades and read up.

Don't go it alone. Lisa's lead carpenter was an essential part of her team because he had deep experience, great contacts, and a willingness to listen and explain. Working with a pro can help fill the gaps in your own experience.

Be prepared. When meeting with building professionals, be on time and bring the necessary paperwork that you need to discuss. A poorly organized project with helpers sitting on their hands will cost you.

Get insured. Licensed contractors must take out liability insurance for all their workers. If you act as your own GC, you must supply that insurance.

Be honest about your abilities. If you're not well organized, patient, and willing to field calls at all hours of the night and day, hire a GC who is.

Cutouts and curves continue on the far end of the big room, culminating in the wavy rail of the sleeping loft. White paint keeps the exposed ceiling lumber from being oppressive. The kitchenette is minimal by design; guests take their meals in the main house.

Lisa and her husband, Michael Hohmeyer, had three sons in seven years. Before having kids, both had active careers and traveled internationally, but now their priorities were at home. Yet they were reluctant to become too isolated. So not long after the birth of their second son, they decided to build some kind of in-law suite so friends from around the world—and of course, grandparents—could come and stay with them.

A cottage wasn't the first option Lisa and Michael thought of. They considered a second-story addition but quickly ruled it out because the complex framing of their hip roof would have been a nightmare to add to. A bump-out attached to the back of the house seemed plausible at first but would have blocked the morning sun and views of the backyard. Eventually, the boys decided it: Though small, they made a prodigious amount of noise. The bigger and noisier they became, the more sense it made to provide a separate place for guests. And there was more than enough room for it in the backyard.

TAKING ON A NEW JOB

The project eventually became far more ambitious than Lisa and Michael had first imagined. If they were going to build a cottage out back, it made sense to landscape the yard at the same time. So the couple decided to develop a master plan for the yard, a new garage (the old one was pretty far gone), and the cottage. Lisa began meeting with Joanne Koch, an architect who

The horizontal wood siding of the cottage is far more informal than the stucco exterior of the big house, here seen across the lawn. Wood siding, run vertically inside the cottage, makes it feel more lighthearted, like a vacation getaway.

Floor Plan

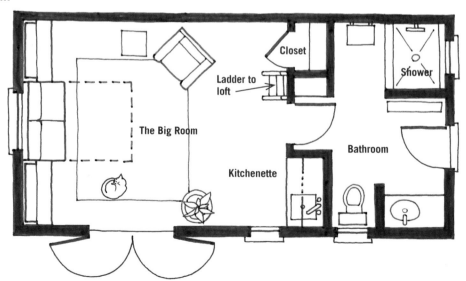

The Big Room

Ladder to loft

Closet

Shower

Bathroom

Kitchenette

had designed an earlier renovation, and a landscape architect. Juiced by the planning sessions, Lisa decided to oversee the project. Thus, a self-described stay-at-home mom became a general contractor.

For most mortals, her decision begs the question, "Why?" Her reasons were both pragmatic and idealistic. Saving the 15-percent markup that GCs typically get was appealing. But perhaps the most compelling reason was a need to be deeply involved in all aspects of design and construction. She missed the tangible satisfaction she had felt at work each time she finished a complicated project. "Being a mother is by far the hardest job I've ever done, but you get hungry for that hit of self-esteem that comes from doing professional work. It's hard to explain, but I know moms will get what I'm talking about."

DELIGHT IN THE DETAILS

As the master plan evolved, the only piece it lacked was someone to do the actual work, and he showed up in the person of Jody Brown, a lead carpenter with great listening skills and a set of patient subs with a collegial way of working.

Dealing directly with Jody, Lisa could make changes fairly easily. As she put it, "We were able to let the design evolve as we were building it." It also

The big room is a mix of playfulness and elegance. Cutout brackets supporting shelves and adorning cabinet bases recall the scrollwork of a beach cottage, while crown molding atop the bookcases and slender caps over window trim add a whiff of formality.

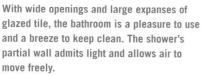

With wide openings and large expanses of glazed tile, the bathroom is a pleasure to use and a breeze to keep clean. The shower's partial wall admits light and allows air to move freely.

Its designer wanted the bathroom to feel like a spa and, indeed, it's often used as a dressing room by day-guests who stop by for a hot tub soak. Light colors and an open plan make the space feel larger than it is.

helped that, inside and out, so much of the cottage was wood: Jody would be the one swinging the hammer. But this fluid arrangement also worked well with the other trades. The shower, for example, was finessed to the inch as Lisa, balancing a baby, figured out the exact width of the shower opening and the height of its curb—low enough to step over but prominent enough that an older person would see it.

It's a great cottage, at once peaceful and playful. The exposed rafters and interior paneling, both painted white, make the big room feel more like a vacation getaway than somebody's backyard. The built-ins and the quirky scrollwork of the trim recall summer cabins in Sweden—or perhaps a very large doll house. Despite all the white trim, though, the interior is warm with sunlight reflected off the honey-colored fir floors, which were sealed with polyurethane to make maintenance easy.

The bathroom is spa-like, with lots of sunlight, gleaming tile, and plenty of room to stretch. You could spend a lot of time in this bathroom. It's downright luxurious, in fact, but somehow works with the rest of the cottage because of a similar color palette and, well, it doesn't take itself too seriously.

The kitchenette is adequate for morning coffee or warming a dish of mac and cheese for visiting sprites but, as the hostess makes clear, the dining room is across that elegant garden, in the big house, with the rest of the family. ☐

The sleeping loft is
a space apart, with
strong diagonals and
dramatic shadows.
White paint keeps all
that big lumber from
being oppressive.

a floating in-law

Charlotte and Michael Green were ready for a change. Bainbridge Island had been a great place to raise kids, but now that the nest was empty, the Greens wanted a more urban lifestyle. One evening while having dinner with friends in Portland, Oregon, they looked across the city and saw, golden in the setting sun, a marina of floating homes.

Minutes from downtown Portland, this eclectic community of floating homes adjoins a peaceful nature preserve. The brown in-law cottage, at center, became the guest house of a larger floating home being built on the other side of the dock.

Floor Plan

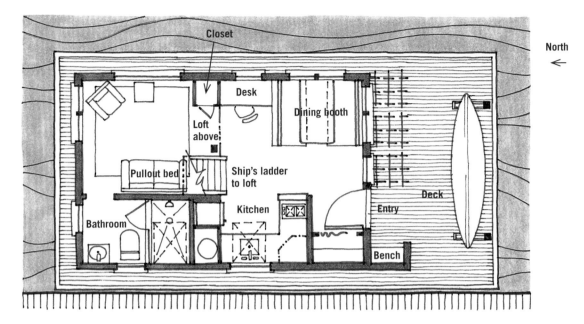

Living on a houseboat appealed to their romantic side, to be sure. But the more they did the math of building a home on the water, the more sense it made. Boat slips were a lot cheaper than building lots. Moreover, if they built an in-law first, they could live on it and see if Portland was a good fit before committing to the big house. (Anyone thinking of relocating can see the wisdom of that.) Few sites on land could match the value, the views, the access to downtown, and the proximity to natural beauty they found in a quiet marina on the Willamette River.

TIPS FOR A TINY FOOTPRINT

One of the few drawbacks of marina living is a lack of space. Each slip has a regulated size that, in turn, dictates the size of the *float* (floating foundation) and the structure you can build on it. Whereas the Greens' main house float was 34 ft. by 70 ft., their *tender* (the in-law unit) float was only 18 ft. by 34 ft. (612 sq. ft.). Once they subtracted space for an 18-in. access clearance around the structure (required by codes) and a modest-size deck, the in-law's footprint was tiny: 433 sq. ft. (see the floor plan above).

Fortunately, the Greens had an ace in the hole—Russ Hamlet, an architect who loves designing small houses. Hamlet believes that if you expand the perceived size of a small house, it won't feel small. His space-expanding tips include:

■ **Have lots of natural light, ideally, from at least two sides.** Don't forget skylights, clerestories, transoms, glass block walls, and small but strategically placed windows.

■ **Create long views.** Whenever possible, avoid doors, stairwell walls, and stair risers (if permitted by code), all of which block views. If you minimize furniture and clutter, your eye will roam even farther.

IF YOUR DECK WILL BE EXPOSED TO A HARSH CLIMATE, consider ipé as your wood. Sustainably grown in South America, ipé is so hard it's sometimes called ironwood. It has a Class-A fire rating and is naturally rot-resistant.

RIGHT: Along the dock side of the houseboat, windows placed high on the kitchen wall protect privacy and a skylight increases natural light. Open shelves are a good solution for small kitchens: You don't have to fight cabinet doors to get at things.

FAR RIGHT: Corner lavatories are a good fit in a tight bathroom. The inset cabinet to the right of the lav likewise takes up very little space, while a custom-built light fixture built into the ceiling unobtrusively lights the mirror.

BELOW: High ceilings, ample windows, and long sight–lines into the loft, the living area below, and the river beyond make the in-law feel spacious and bright.

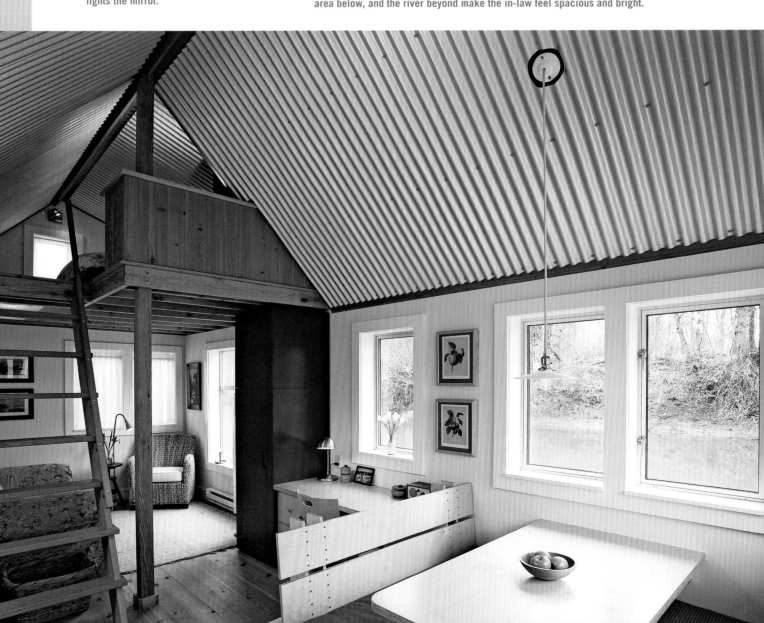

METAL-FRAMED WINDOWS HAVE THINNER MUNTINS than wood windows, so they block less of the view, and they have a clean, modern look. But if you're put off by the heat metal windows lose, consider thermal-break versions, which have a better e-rating.

- **Multipurpose your rooms.** Accommodate activities that don't occur at the same time, such as dining tables that double as desks and Murphy beds in living rooms.
- **Contrast light and color.** Light colors and reflective surfaces expand space. Dark ones enclose space and make it feel cozy.
- **Create zones.** Even small houses need public areas and private ones such as the loft.
- **Vary scale.** Used selectively, oversized windows, high ceilings, thick counter edges, tall columns, and other big-house elements can make little houses feel grand.
- **Live outdoors.** Decks and patios are just rooms without walls or ceilings.
- **Watch the elbows.** Rethink any space so small that you bang your elbows in it. You shouldn't feel uncomfortable in your own home.

The sleeping loft is accessed by a steep ship's ladder (photo above), with an extended rail at the top to provide improved safety. The loft (top photo) has some of the fun of a kid's hideaway. With dormer windows looking east, it's a great place to watch ducks, turtles, beaver, bald eagles, and osprey. The steel ceiling shimmers with light off the water.

TRY-OUTS FOR THE BIG HOUSE

After a year of staying on their floating in-law and exploring Portland, Charlotte and Michael took the plunge and began work on the main houseboat. In addition to allowing them to explore the area, building the in-law first

enabled the Greens to experiment with materials they might want to use in the main house such as galvanized metal countertops, recycled wood floors, and a corrugated metal ceiling that reflects light off the river. It also offered the opportunity to try out unusual details, such as the custom-built recessed light fixture in the bathroom (see the drawing below).

The Greens are quick to emphasize, however, that the main house will look very different from the in-law. The in-law was designed, after all, as a guesthouse, deliberately cute and romantic. Charlotte adds, "When the main house is finished, we'll still go over there every now and then to spend a night in the loft. Especially in summer when we can throw open the windows and listen to the water and the sounds of the wildlife. It's another world over there." ☐

The shower pan of this stall is simply a thin skim coat of concrete over the cottage's floating foundation. Green glass tiles refract and reflect the light.

ONE OF THE FEW DOWNSIDES OF A SKYLIGHT is that it looks like a black hole in the ceiling at night. If, however, you place a small spotlight inside the frame of a skylight, at night it will illuminate the room from the same direction as daylight. Put it on a dimmer switch for mood lighting.

Built-in Light Fixture

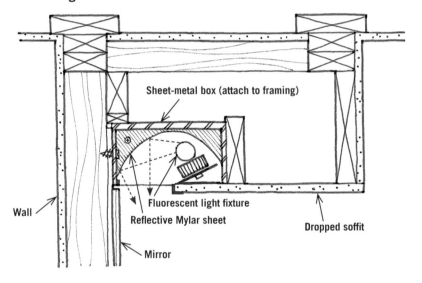

Sheet-metal box (attach to framing)

Fluorescent light fixture

Reflective Mylar sheet

Wall

Mirror

Dropped soffit

LIVING IN CLOSE QUARTERS

Living in a marina—or in an in-law with a tiny shared yard—is a bit like living in another culture, but once you adapt to the local customs you'll be more comfortable. Because marina walkways run close by individual houseboats, for example, the Greens learned not to start a conversation with neighbors sitting outdoors unless that person first made eye contact. Playing music loud was also taboo.

Living in close quarters has its upsides, though. Everyone knows everyone else and there's a nice community feeling. Though people respect one another's privacy, they look out for one another. If someone is absent during a severe storm, neighbors will check the houseboat for damage or shovel snow off a roof. People rarely move on and anyone living there will tell you it's like being on vacation every day.

Twilight on the Willamette River.

rooting for a green world

The most remarkable thing about Lisa's in-law studio is not its sod-covered roof, though that's often what visitors notice first. More remarkable is that in 200 sq. ft.—smaller than a one-car garage—Lisa has an office, a conference area, a guest studio with a queen bed, a half bath, and a showcase of green building practices. This studio is not, admittedly, a full-bore in-law unit, but it's a marvel of how small small can be—and still be nice.

Lisa and her partner, Ken, weren't thinking *green* when they first considered building an in-law. They were thinking comfort. Every time friends and family came to stay, Ken got kicked out of his study, which had a sofa bed. (One German cousin stayed six months.) In response, the couple thought of converting a funky, powder-post-beetle infested workshop on their property into a guest cottage, but dropped the idea because renovating it or changing its use would have triggered a zoning review (see Chapter 4).

RECYCLED DENIM IS NOT ONLY GOOD INSULATION, it's excellent for sound-proofing walls. Far denser than fiberglass, it deadens sound. Denim batts are tedious to cut with a utility knife, however; an electric turkey-carving knife is the tool of choice.

Floor Plan

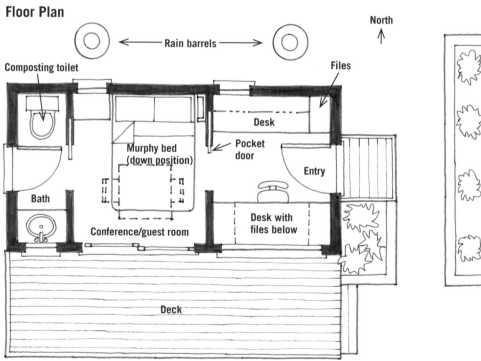

North

Rain barrels

Composting toilet

Files

Desk

Murphy bed (down position)

Pocket door

Entry

Bath

Desk with files below

Conference/guest room

Deck

Clad in corrugated metal siding and a sod roof, this guest studio/office (photo above) fits easily in an eclectic neighborhood on Bainbridge Island. When it is fully grown, a stand of bamboo will screen the parking area from the office. Its sod roof (photo right) helps the building to blend into the landscape.

Adding on to their two-bedroom house was out because it would have looked like a hodgepodge and upset the scale of their quiet island community. So a decade passed, during which time green building grew up. Finally, in 2008, Lisa contacted a local architect, Russ Hamlet, to design a studio that could house guests and serve as her office.

BUILDING LIGHTLY ON THE LAND

Hamlet was a neighbor, so he had a good sense of what would be right for an area whose hedgerows, winding footpaths, and close-by houses feel almost English. He suggested locating the studio midway up the sloping lot, at a right angle to the workshop. With the main house, the buildings would form a snug compound. The only drawback was that the new studio would intrude slightly

South-facing windows provide passive solar gain and views to the house and Puget Sound in the distance. The walls are insulated with recycled denim, and all windows are doubled glazed.

on an uphill neighbor's view of Puget Sound. Hamlet's solution to that problem was about as green as green gets.

Enter the sod roof (see the sidebar below). Covered with vegetation, the roof would recede into the landscape, greatly pleasing the uphill neighbor. It also would modestly reduce storm water runoff into the sound (runoff pollution is a huge issue on the island). Everybody loved the idea, so Hamlet pushed on. Because the building had a small footprint and didn't weigh much, it could sit on concrete piers formed by Sonotubes®. Hence, no impermeable slab or stemwall foundation, no perimeter drains, and no dank crawlspaces. A composting toilet would further reduce the studio's impact on the land, as would semi-permeable brick walkways and gravel parking spaces.

Above ground, a host of alternative building materials conserve resources. Large south-facing thermal windows let in so much natural light that even on gray days Lisa rarely turns on the low-voltage halogens on the ceiling or the recessed LED lights over the desk. There's also solar gain, of course, and that, combined with sod insulation on the roof and recycled denim insulation in the walls, makes for miserly energy consumption. A single wall-mounted electric convection heater can heat the entire space. In summer, the generous roof overhang shades the studio and deck. Recyclable composite decking, salvaged jatoba flooring, and locally sourced Douglas fir paneling certified by the FSC (Forest Stewardship Council) complete the array of secondhand and sustainable materials.

THE SPECIFICS OF SOD

Even in mild climates, a rooftop can be an arid, inhospitable environment. Successfully planting a sod roof takes attention to detail and, most important, knowledge of local soils and plants. Because soil can be heavy—especially during the wet months—a sod roof is typically only 3 in. to 4 in. thick. Scouring winds and searing sun can shrink soil, so gritty soil mixtures high in minerals and low in organic content seem to work best. (Bonsai trees are planted in similar mixtures.)

In terms of plants, the heartiest rooftop specimens are *sedums*, small succulents with shallow roots that come in many colors. They can withstand heat and don't need much water once they're established. Sod-roof experts suggest planting the sedums densely to avoid bare spots and to crowd out weeds. You'll need to water a fair amount and weed now and then the first season, but beyond that, sod roofs can be largely maintenance-free. Always seek local expertise for construction details, soils, and plants appropriate for your area.

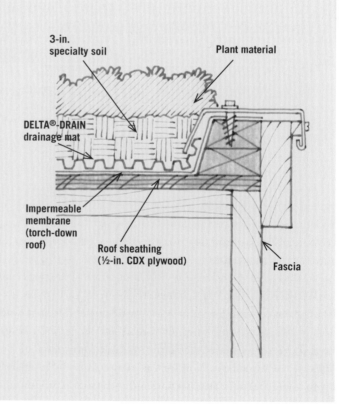

When there are no guests, the large room adjacent to the office (photo above) doubles as a conference area. The energy-efficient electric convection heater mounted to the wall, lower left, can heat the entire studio. When the Murphy bed is lowered (photo at right), the room becomes a comfortable sleeping area. The pocket door can be locked to secure the office from the guest room.

Best of all, when guests come to stay, Ken and Lisa can keep working. The east end of the structure is a dedicated office with built-in desks large enough to spread out blueprints (see the photo on the facing page). When there are no guests, Lisa uses the adjoining room as a conference area to meet with clients. And when visitors are in residence, the Murphy bed comes down. Then the pocket door between the office and guest suite slides shut (and locks), and Lisa can hunker down in her office. For meals and hanging out, everyone retires to the main house. It's a comfortable setup all around, and for Lisa and her blossoming eco-development land company, there's the added benefit of seeing how well alternative materials and methods work, firsthand. □

nancy's windfall

For some time, Nancy Stein had been thinking about building an in-law she could rent out. Her daughter would be starting college in a few years and the income seemed a good way to create a nest egg for her schooling. Providing affordable housing for a local person also seemed a worthwhile thing to do in a rural area with few rentals at any price.

But Nancy could never quite make the numbers work. "I work as a gardener and an artist and don't have any money," she noted. "My father left a small sum when he died but with seven kids splitting it, it wasn't much. Even with my sweat equity thrown in, I had about half what I needed to make it happen."

Then, one black night during a howling storm, good fortune arrived with a thundering crash.

Almost all the wood in this 450-sq.-ft. cabin came from a single tree that fell a short distance away. The driveway to the main house runs close by, so on that side of the cottage there is only a tiny roofed window. Except for a rhododendron planted by the owner, Mother Nature did all the landscaping.

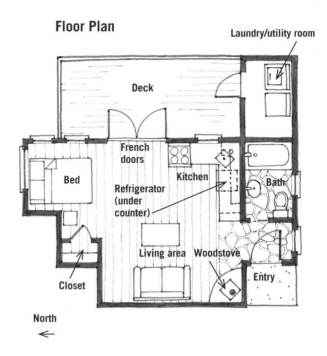

Floor Plan

Laundry/utility room

Deck

French doors

Kitchen

Bed

Refrigerator (under counter)

Bath

Living area

Woodstove

Closet

Entry

North

ABOVE, LEFT: A weathered, hand-painted pocket door lends personality and makes the cabin seem as if it's been there for ages. The flagstone foyer, on the other hand, offers durability. Because flagstone—quartzite veneer, to be exact—is indestructible, you can feed the woodstove or unload groceries without having to take off your shoes.

THE TREE THAT BUILT A HOUSE

Weakened by a gale that had blown all day, an immense fir tree on the ridge suddenly snapped like a giant wooden match. Its top half smacked the ground so hard that a hundred yards away Nancy felt her house bounce. That may sound like a tall tale, but it was a lot of tree. When Nancy and a logger walked the property a few days later, they found that the downed Douglas fir had stood 130 ft. tall and measured nearly 5 ft. across the base. After sawing through it and counting its rings, they discovered that the tree was 98 years old and in the pink of health. There was no rot. The winds had simply overpowered it.

The fir was so big, in fact, that you could build a small house from it. In short order, Nancy found a local builder with a knack for making small spaces charming and livable, swapped services with a local architect, roughed out a set of plans, and had the fir milled on-site into just about every piece of wood she would need.

"I used every stick of that tree," she explained. She knew she wanted to build a modified post and beam building, so the first step was to identify the largest timbers, then the framing lumber such as joists and rafters and so on, right down to the siding, flooring, and ceiling boards. Some of the wood became furniture, and the smaller branches and debris were saved for kindling. The bark was turned into mulch.

AT HOME IN THE WOODS

On a wooded slope not far from where the tree went down, they raised the cottage (see the floor plan, above). Clad in board-and-batten siding stained gray, it's right at home. A modest overhang provides shelter from the wet while you fish for your house keys. And if you return home with muddy boots, no matter. A durable expanse of flagstone flooring just inside the door allows

ABOVE: The kitchen is complete but compact. The undercounter refrigerator won't hold more than a few days' supply of fruits and vegetables. But that's a virtue in a farming area that has fresh organic produce available most of the year.

The flagstone continues into the bathroom and up the tub surround.

INSULATING DOWN UNDER

Though most of Nancy's cottage sits on a full foundation, its cantilevered sections needed extra insulation to keep the floors warm. This was achieved by installing two layers of 3-in. Thermax™ rigid polyisocyanurate insulation panels snug against the underside of the subfloor. To stop air leaks, panel joints were staggered and sprayed with expanding foam. To keep critters from nesting in the insulation, the contractor stapled ½-in.-square galvanized hardware cloth to the underside of joists, which also helped keep things well ventilated and dry.

access to the bathroom, the woodstove, and the edge of the kitchen. Muddy boots that would destroy wood floors don't phase flagstone. Thanks to this thoughtful detail, the floors look like they were installed yesterday.

The cabin is warm and seems spacious. Because it was carefully insulated (including the floors), a handful of kindling has it toasty in 10 or 15 minutes. There are electric baseboard heaters as a backup but tenants rarely use them. The ruddy hue of the fir boards and timber also adds to the warm feeling, giving the soft sunlight a faintly peach cast. So much exposed wood might have been oppressive, so Nancy finished it with a diluted white stain to lighten it.

The cabin's tiny footprint seems expanded by its high ceilings. A windowless wall to the west is offset by fully glazed French doors to the east that open onto a deck, a lordly vista, and sun that filters through the morning fog. The jogged floor plan (see the drawing on p. 167) is an especially clever way to create long sight lines and define the different uses of the space without chopping it up. When you lie in bed, surrounded by an alcove of windows, you feel like you're in another room—or living high in the air. It's about as close to nature as you can get without being outside.

LIVING IN THE AIR

The living is easy outside, too. When the weather is nice, there's a grand deck where you can catch some rays, take in the views, or grill dinner. With both French doors thrown open, the living space is just about doubled. Whatever the season, the deck is a prime perch for watching nature: there's always something stirring in the forest or floating in the air.

"This place has a wonderful wild feeling to it that I wanted to share with people who would appreciate it," Nancy reflects. "It's had a great affect on the lives of people who have lived here. Several people came to heal or find solace from stressful lives. Some tenants cocoon and don't interact much and that's fine. Good friendships often take time. You see each other coming and going, you stop to chat, you get to know each other slowly.

"I feel incredibly blessed. The tree falling, this sweet cottage, the healing that happens here, the friendships—it's all a gift." □

ABOVE: Small though it is, the tiny window in the roof oozes charm and bathes the room in warm afternoon light. The cottage is wonderfully cozy, especially when it's raw outside. Once warmed, the flagstone surround behind the stove radiates heat even after the fire has gone out.

LEFT: Creating a space that's both majestic and intimate is quite a feat. After the cottage had stood for ten years, one day the owner realized that if she bumped out the wall at the head of the bed and wrapped it with windows, she could create an alcove that separated the bedroom space from the rest of the room.

a new life for an elderly in-law

This 1917 cottage had serious structural problems and zoning issues that had to be resolved before it could be rehabbed.

BELOW: The cottage, reborn. With a new foundation, reinforced framing, new wiring and plumbing, double-glazed windows, energy-saving appliances, and a floor plan that makes use of every inch, this in-law is ready for its second century.

When the Shaws first saw the roomy two-story Victorian house, it seemed a perfect fit. They particularly liked the in-law cottage in back because it could become a home for Don's mother, who had been circulating among her kids' houses for several years. The in-law needed work but Mother could stay in the big house until the work was complete—in six months, max, they were assured. So, with one eye on their bank balance and the other on the calendar, the Shaws settled in under one roof and the cottage renovation began. They soon found, however, that renovation projects are always unpredictable, especially when they involve an old place with a lot of deferred maintenance. So if you're rehabbing an in-law so mom or pop can move in, better wait till the paint is dry before calling the moving van.

Outbuildings constructed at the turn of the twentieth century were underbuilt by modern standards, but it was a wonder that the Shaws' cottage was still standing. When their contractor opened up the walls, he found not 2x4 studs spaced 16 in. on-center (o.c.), but 2x3 studs 24 in. to 36 in. apart. Even stranger, the original carpenter had placed the studs flat rather than on-edge, creating a thinner and far less supportive wall. The apex of his odd methods, however, was the roof framing: 2x4 rafters spaced 36 in. o.c. In a stiff wind the roof must have billowed like a tent.

IF WOOD SHINGLES HAVE BEEN ON THE ROOF for more than 20 years and require widespread repairs, it's time to re-roof. Likewise, if shingle siding needs extensive patching, strip and replace the whole exterior. Otherwise, you'll be patching it till the end of time.

Floor Plan

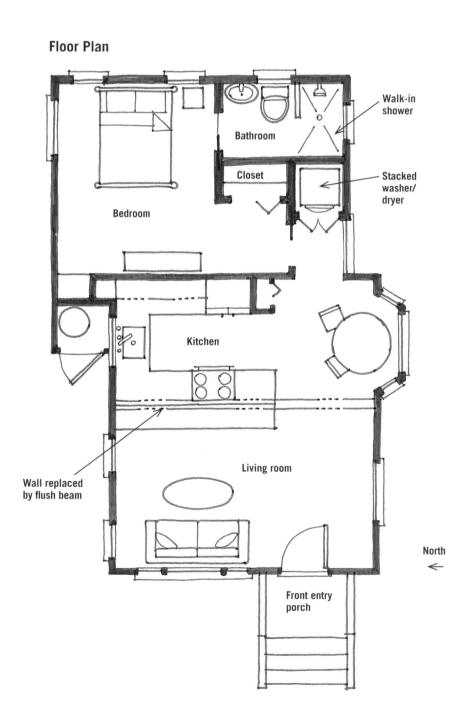

Walk-in shower

Bathroom

Closet

Stacked washer/dryer

Bedroom

Kitchen

Wall replaced by flush beam

Living room

North

Front entry porch

Though it uses some modern materials to cut costs—such as laminate counters and prefab cabinets—the renovation faithfully re-creates an Arts and Crafts feeling. The beadboard ceiling is original.

HIDING A BEAM

Joists usually sit on top of a beam, but *flush beams* are different: Joists hang from the sides of a flush beam, supported by metal joist hangers. That means the bottom edge of the beam can be flush with the bottom edges of the joists, so it won't show when the ceiling is covered with drywall. Flush beams are favored where a designer wants a large expanse of open space unencumbered by a beam or supporting wall, or where an exposed beam would make the ceiling too low.

A HAND FROM THE PAST

Like many old buildings, the Shaw cottage sat too close to the rear property line. So when architect Jerri Holan contacted the planning department about rehabbing the cottage, she was given two options: Relocate it to suit current setbacks, or find the original permit to prove that it had been legally built where it stood. The cottage was so funky that relocating it wasn't viable, and the second option was a long shot. In the old days, owners rarely bothered with permits for in-laws, they just built them. With a lot of digging and equal amounts of luck, however, Holan found the original permit. It was issued in 1917 to J. Hasky, who had taken the trouble to pay fifty cents for a building permit for an in-law that cost $5 to build. Thus, because it was legal, the cottage could be renovated where it stood.

OPENING UP NEW POSSIBILITIES

At 537 sq. ft., the cottage was small but Holan and the Shaws decided to work with the existing footprint to avoid a lengthy design-review process and any further delay. The job was already behind schedule and the big house was feeling smaller by the day.

The first order of business was to replace the old foundation and add drainage and a sump pump, followed by beefing up the cottage's undersize framing. It would have been easier to tear down the old frame, but demolishing more than 50 percent of the structure would have triggered regulations that required the building to conform to current setbacks. Having dodged that bullet during the design phase, the building crew wasn't taking any chances. In the end, the contractor decided to bolster the old joists, studs, and rafters by adding new framing between them.

While the foundation work was under way, Holan and her design team were juggling the modern needs of an older person with the aesthetics of an Arts and Crafts cottage. To bring light into the small, dark cottage, their plan removed the bearing wall between the kitchen and the living room and installed a flush beam, creating a large, open space.

Then they added a south-facing bay window to expand the kitchen and create a sunny eating nook, transformed a small back porch into a laundry room, squared off the bedroom, and added built-in shelves typical of the period. Finally, in a burst of inspired efficiency, they scrapped the tiny bathroom dominated by a water heater, installed an on-demand water heater

To open up space and bring more light into the cottage, a wall between the kitchen and the living room was replaced with a flush beam hidden in the ceiling.

HOT WHEN YOU NEED IT

An on-demand water heater costs considerably more initially than a standard water heater but saves in the end, especially in temperate climates. Properly configured, it can supply hot water for both potable water and heating systems. It can be mounted to a building's exterior in mild climates but will fit nicely on an interior wall. Either way it saves precious floor space.

outside, and, with the space they freed up, created a sunny barrier-free bathroom in a corner of the in-law that had previously lacked any view.

By the time the project got to finish stages, almost a year had elapsed. Inside the cottage, its 1917 charm was starting to return. With a lot of caulk, the original beadboard ceiling was restored. Salvaged panel doors, heavy casings, period lighting throughout, and 3 in. by 6 in. bathroom tiles were all faithful to the bungalow's Art and Crafts roots.

The few concessions to an overstrained budget looked pretty good, too. Laminate maple flooring instead of real hardwood, white laminate countertops in lieu of tile, and prefab Shaker-style kitchen cabinets all helped salvage the budget. On one final touch, the Shaws splurged, adding a pair of leaded-glass windows in the living room.

Four months later than planned, Mother moved into the cottage and loved it from the first day. When it's sunny she works in the garden, when it's inclement she reads on the porch, and most evenings, she dines in the big house and catches up on the day's doings. □

ABOVE: Tiny but light-filled, the bedroom looks out onto gardens side and back.

RIGHT: Understated and efficient, this ADA-compliant bathroom won several national awards for ease of access and use. Because it has neither thresholds or curbs, it presents no barriers to someone in a walker or a wheelchair.

elegance under the oaks

O ver the years, Suzie McKig and her mother, Billie, had often discussed some kind of dual living setup they might try when Billie got older, but it never quite happened. Billie had an active social life and a big house in San Diego, and Suzie's kids and her graphic design business in Los Angeles consumed her waking hours. Then, in the course of a year, Suzie got remarried, decided to move her business, and found a house in Berkeley with a backyard big enough for a cottage.

The large backyard will someday be a garden shared by both households. Protected by the city, the live oaks on the property almost thwarted the cottage's construction.

OPPOSITE: Facing the
garden, the intimate eating
alcove feels removed from
the kitchen.

Filtered through glass
blocks, the morning sun
bathes the shower in warm
light. Throughout the day,
the bathroom has a subtle
luminescence.

LIVE AND LET LIVE

As more and more cities protect legacy trees, homeowners wanting to build
in-laws may face restrictions similar to the McKigs': You can't kill trees to
build a house. To find a way to build within the drip-line without disturbing
tree roots, architect John Hopkins enlisted a licensed arborist, a structural
engineer, and a city planner. The solution all three agreed with was a
foundation of above-grade concrete beams that sat atop several concrete
piers (see the drawings below).

This approach required no excavation other than digging individual piers.
The builder dug holes where the plan indicated; if he encountered a root,
he stopped and dug nearby until he found a clear space. Today, the oak is
thriving and now shields the cottage from the harsh afternoon sun.

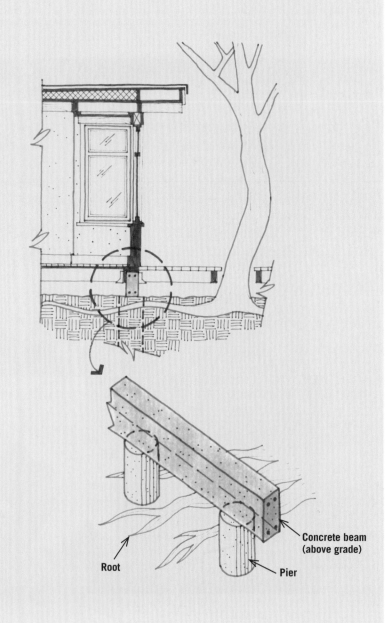

Root

Concrete beam
(above grade)

Pier

TAKING ROOT IN THE BACKYARD

So, in the midst of big life changes all around, Billie moved into Suzie's new place and, shortly, architect John Hopkins began designing Billie's cottage in the backyard. Billie was pretty clear about what she needed: lots of windows and light, high ceilings, a decent-size bathroom, a living room large enough to entertain a few friends comfortably, and a fireplace. Had to have a fireplace.

It was a modest list, but the architect's skills were put to the test by two stringent city requirements: The cottage footprint could be no more than 540 sq. ft. and its foundation could not be located within the drip-line of a large live oak that stood on the most logical building site. Fortunately a clever solution saved both the tree (see the photo on p. 181) and the cottage.

SMALL BUT COMMODIOUS

To make the most of the project's small footprint, the plan Hopkins devised eliminates halls, a formal entry, stairs, and other space wasters (see the floor plan below). He settled on two commodious, multipurpose rooms. The main room accommodates kitchen, dining, and living functions—all with good sightlines into the garden and a view of the fireplace. He placed a dining alcove along the front windows. Separated from the main room by a door, the bedroom is the cottage's private space, with an adjoining bath and a walk-in closet that doubles as a laundry.

This multi-functionality wouldn't have been possible without compact appliances. The kitchen houses a refrigerator and range, each 2 ft. wide, a

Floor Plan

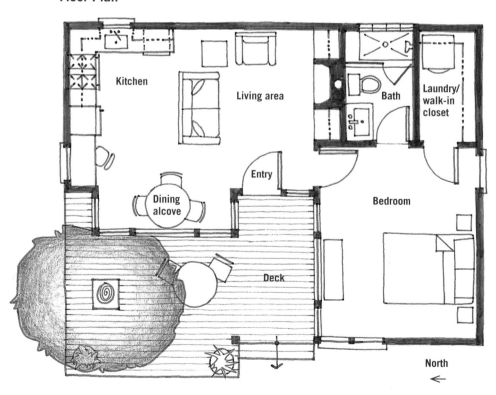

ABOVE: Compact appliances, base cabinets on slender legs, and light-colored wood finishes give this kitchen a low profile in a shared space. No single use dominates the area.

Red cedar beams, custom built-ins, and a stone fireplace surround make the living area feel luxurious. High ceilings and ceiling-to-floor windows make it feel spacious. The gas fireplace is the cottage's sole heat source.

single-bowl sink that frees up counter space, and a single-drawer dishwasher. In the bedroom closet, a dual-function washer-dryer takes so little space that there's room above it for six shelves. Even the in-law's mechanical equipment is space-conserving: a tankless water heater is mounted to an outside wall, and the gas fireplace in the living room (controlled by a thermostat) is sufficient to heat the well-insulated cottage in the mild northern California climate.

High ceilings are an important part of making the small cottage feel big but Hopkins almost ran afoul of zoning requirements that the cottage be no more than 12 ft. tall. The above-grade foundation meant a raised floor, and that ate into the allowable 12-ft. height. By using pressure-treated framing to lower the height of the crawlspace, however, the design team was able to eke out an 8-ft., 9-in. ceiling. That height, combined with an 8-ft.-tall front door and ganged windows, makes Billie's place feel very spacious. Indeed, she comfortably entertains eight or ten friends with some regularity.

THE COLOR OF INDEPENDENCE

With exposed red-cedar ceiling and matching eaves, Douglas fir 4x6 rafters and matching windows, doors, and trim—to say nothing of its bamboo floors—Billie's cottage is alive with color. Suzie also applied her keen designer's eye inside and out. The bedroom has four subtle hues of apple green and the cottage exterior is compatible with the colors of the deck, the garden, and the main house. Suzie is quick to point out, though, that Billie had final say, "It's her home, not an extension of ours. When someone is as independent as my mom, she should feel in every way that her home reflects her." □

GET OUT AND MAKE FRIENDS when you relocate to a new area to live with your kids. It's too easy to fall into the trap of being dependent on your family, especially for an older person. Meet people so you can have a life of your own.

FACING PAGE AND BELOW: Thanks to the Bay Area's mild climate, the deck can be used most of the year, effectively doubling the living space of the cottage. A live oak frames the entrance and shades the cottage from the harsh afternoon sun.

CHAPTER 8

bump-outs, carve-outs, and attics

BUMP-OUTS HAVE GREAT APPEAL because they conserve yard space and, because they adjoin the house, there's one less wall to build. If you want to create a living space for an elderly parent or a caregiver, they'll be right on the other side of the wall.

Carve-outs are even more intimate. Created by carving out a suite of rooms within a house, they are the least expensive and least disruptive type of in-law to build. Close off an interior door or two, add soundproofing, install a kitchenette, and, voilà!, a second home.

Living in an attic in-law can be a great adventure for the right person. Sloping roofs, skylights, quirky nooks, and long views create an inherently romantic, cozy living space. Because of the stairs involved, though, such units are probably best suited to a younger person, or at least someone with strong legs and a good back.

a jewel in the city

A s cities get denser and zoning regulations become more restrictive, homeowners who want to add on will have to become more resourceful when dealing with planning and building departments and more creative in solving problems. Fortunately, as Art and Susan Hartinger learned, severe constraints can sometimes lead to stunning designs.

ABOVE: The Hartinger's old garage was an improvised affair with a deck on top, tacked onto a Craftsman bungalow. Built on one of the tiniest lots in town, the house had no other place in which to add an in-law unit.

The rebuilt garage and its in-law look original. This subtle effect was achieved by matching the colors, trim style, and roof pitch of the main house, aligning siding courses, subordinating the renovation to the house, and setting it well back from the street.

The Hartingers and their two daughters lived in a cozy 1912 Craftsman bungalow with two bedrooms and one bath. When the girls were small, there was room enough, but when they became teens and sharing a bedroom became untenable, one of the girls moved into the sleeping porch Art had used as a study. Art, an attorney, often works at home, so after being displaced, he and his papers migrated to other rooms. According to Susan, "When he was working on a case, he took over the house. His stuff was everywhere."

The Hartingers briefly considered developing the attic or raising the house to add a floor underneath, but either option would have been disruptive, costly, and would probably have destroyed the bungalow's intimate charm. Instead, the Hartingers hired architect Steve Rynerson to design a small bump-out suite over the garage that could serve as a guest room and a study for Art, with a full bath to alleviate the morning traffic jam outside the family's one full bathroom.

A MODEST PROPOSAL FOR A TINY LOT

Located near a flatiron corner created by two diagonally intersecting streets, the lot was the smallest on the block, and it backed up to the smallest lot on the adjoining street. ("You could eat watermelon on the back deck and spit seeds into the neighbors' backyard," says Art.) The house was already *nonconforming* (see the sidebar on p. 10) in two respects: It covered too much of the lot and was too close to property lines. Given those conditions,

ALWAYS TRY TO BE INFORMED, polite, and helpful when dealing with the building inspectors or city planners assigned to your project. If the relationship becomes unworkable, you can request to have another person assigned. But be *very* well prepared when you make that request.

Floor Plan

The back of the suite contains a full bathroom with a pocket door, a storage closet next to a door that opens onto a small landing, and a sleeping loft. When not in use, the loft ladder hangs on a wall cleat.

Rynerson was uncertain how the city would view an addition so he worked up a preliminary design and took it to the planning department.

The planner whom Rynerson met with wouldn't say yes or no. The city's position was, essentially, fully develop a design and then we'll let you know whether we'll approve it. It was a risk, but because Susan and Art loved their house and a white-hot housing market was pricing comparable properties out of reach, they decided to go ahead with the plans for the bump-out.

Refining the Hartingers' design became a question of how much use could be shoehorned into a limited space—less than 250 sq. ft. They found that by creating a sleeping loft, the suite could accommodate a full (if tight) bathroom, a closet, and a study. Moreover, a loft tall enough to stand up in would have

Skillful staining gives this new board-and-batten paneling the same 100-year-old glow found in the rest of the house. The low shelves at left create a little vestibule that lends privacy and eases the transition from the dining room in the main house.

great views to the west. After working out the details, Rynerson submitted a full set of plans to the city, which then sent a planner out to the site.

This time, the Hartingers didn't have to wait for an answer: It was no. The planner denied their proposal because, she maintained, even an addition as modest as theirs would be too close to the rear neighbor. She came to this conclusion even though the Hartingers had submitted letters from all their near neighbors when they applied for a permit; none had objected. Moreover, there was no evidence that such an addition would block anyone's views or sunlight.

To say the least, the Hartingers and Rynerson were shocked.

APPEALING THE DECISION

But Art Hartinger, for one, wasn't buying the planner's argument. As an attorney, he knew that cities routinely allow owners of older, nonconforming properties to add on as long as the addition doesn't aggravate the nonconforming conditions—and the Hartinger proposal didn't. Moreover, in almost a century, the house had never had a major addition, unlike many houses in the neighborhood. The Hartingers began enlisting the support of neighbors, lobbying their councilman, and drafting an appeal to the city council, which has the final say in such disputes.

Fortunately, the dispute never went to a hearing. The Hartingers were able to reach a compromise. In return for having their plans approved, they agreed to reduce the height of the second floor by about 4 ft.—creating a sit-up loft rather than a stand-up loft—and to move the bulk of the loft area slightly away from the rear property line.

At the end of the day, though, the Hartingers got far more than they had to give, and the suite is quite a stunner. Its Craftsman details are so faithfully reproduced that guests are usually shocked to learn that it's new. When the sun streams in, the room feels somewhat like a chapel. And in addition to a loft with views of San Francisco Bay, the suite has built-in bookcases wrapping three walls, solid oak floors, wood paneling up to the roofline, and a jewel of a bathroom. "I love that bathroom," says Susan with a thrill in her voice. "If you have the porthole open, it's almost like an outdoor shower." □

ABOVE: Thanks to neighboring trees all around, the deck for the main house in back feels both expansive and private. The deck is easily accessed from the in-law unit's back stairs.

BELOW, LEFT: The Hartingers are avid sailors so a tiny bathroom is nothing new. Created by master tiler Riley Doty, the bathroom is a subtle mix of greens and blues running throughout the tile, the stone countertop, and the pebbled shower pan. To catch errant spray, the whole floor is tiled. The tiny sink features a faucet angled to save space and a built-in towel bar.

BELOW, RIGHT: The double awning window has glass in the sash that opens out and an old-fashioned wood-framed screen on the sash opening in. The towel hook was set high in order to allow a large towel to hang from it without interfering with the counter.

sailors' delight

The in-law, at right, coexists nicely with the main house, sharing exterior colors, common siding, a roof overhang, and a brick courtyard. Set in sand, the bricks create a permeable surface that rain can drain through, a welcome detail in a climate with wet winters.

Long before small was beautiful and houses were "not so big," there were sailors. More than almost anybody, sailors know about making the most of small spaces because boats, like fish, must be streamlined. Nothing delights sailors more than showing off seats that fold into beds, or postage-stamp galleys that can turn out a ten-course meal. That attitude led two sailors to design and build an in-law unit that does everything but float.

When Beth and Gary Sumner aren't sailing, they live in Eugene, Oregon, where they own an art and architectural stained-glass studio. Gary bought a single-story house there in 1978. At first, they housed the studio in the bump-out that had been a single-car garage, but they eventually rented a warehouse. Then, one day, they realized that their kids were grown and gone and that two bedrooms and the 360 sq. ft. studio were sitting idle.

So the Sumners decided to convert the studio into an in-law for themselves and rent out the three-bedroom main house. "Gary and I kid that we're self-unemployed," Beth laughed, "because everything we have is tied up in the business. Renting the main house made sense because it saves money and frees us to travel. Plus, we were curious to see if we could get along in such a small space."

Speck, the Sumner's first love and their inspiration to live compactly on land.

Floor Plan

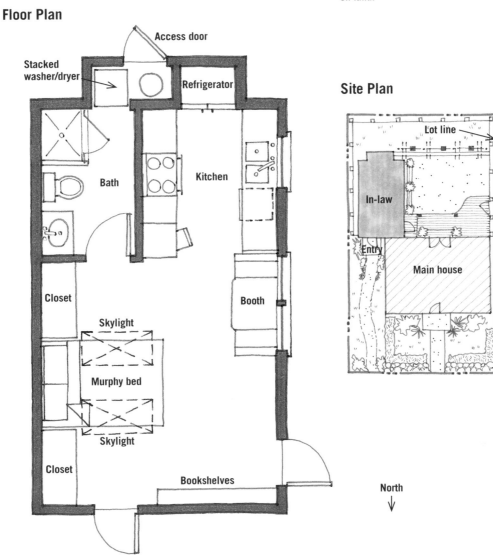

- Access door
- Stacked washer/dryer
- Refrigerator
- Bath
- Kitchen
- Closet
- Booth
- Skylight
- Murphy bed
- Skylight
- Closet
- Bookshelves

Site Plan

- Lot line
- In-law
- Entry
- Main house

North ↓

BOLSTERING AN OLD ROOF

The good old days weren't all good. Old roofs were often framed with 2x4 rafters, which invariably sagged. If, like the Sumners, you must leave an old roof in place, consider their solution: Bolster those 2x4 rafters with 2x6s underneath—creating, in effect, 2x10s that stiffen the roof plane so it doesn't sag. Deeper rafters can accommodate deeper insulation and, as important, provide room for ventilation channels above the insulation to vent hot air and moisture vapor.

The original roof couldn't be disturbed, so workers supported it with steel girders while replacing the old concrete floor slab and then building walls up to the roof.

PLANNING AN IN-LAW CAN BE COMPLICATED and stressful. If you come to an impasse with a partner on the project, don't fight . . . sit tight. Revisit the disputed point in a day or two. And if time doesn't do the trick, ask a mutual friend for advice.

Before sketching a layout, Beth and Gary drew up a short list of requirements:

- **No clutter.** The couple applied this rule whenever they were uncertain about a design choice. There are no floor or table lamps, for example, and only two movable chairs in the unit—one rocker and a computer chair. They used built-ins wherever possible.
- **Nice details.** The Sumners knew a number of high-end woodworkers, so the windows and doors are clear-grain fir and the custom cabinets are rift-cut white oak. Not surprising, there's also a lot of stained glass.
- **Open and bright.** This requirement led to two important design choices: a cathedral ceiling whose peak is almost 12 ft. high and skylights that open.
- **Full-size kitchen appliances and a roomy shower.** Shipboard cooking and showering are cramped affairs so this is one instance where comfort trumped compact. The Sumners cook a lot so they wanted a stove and refrigerator up to the task as well as enough room for both of them in the kitchen. And there's no nicer antidote to salt-encrusted skin or sandy hair than a blasting hot shower for as long as you like: They installed a 50-gal. water heater.

DESIGN SQUEEZE

Beth and Gary's project had a number of constraints, the first of which was the small lot size. The house and studio were built in 1936, before zoning regulations, so the structures were quite close to property lines on the east and west sides of the lot and their combined square footage far exceeded the allowable lot coverage. To retain the grandfather status (see the sidebar on p. 10) of the studio, the Sumners had to work within the existing footprint and retain the original roof. The roof framing, however, had to be strengthened (see the sidebar, above).

The north end of the in-law was attached to the house, sharing a 6-ft. section of common wall. That end also contained a door that had to stay because it provided access to a covered driveway. The local building code required two exterior doors, so they located the second one where the buildings intersect; the generous overhang of the house would protect the door from rain.

Beth and Gary first considered putting the kitchen in the north end of the in-law, but two things argued against that. First, they wanted to be good

ABOVE: Everything has its place. A built-in desk sits next to oak doors hiding the Murphy bed. At left, a bookcase covers the soundproofed wall between the house and the in-law.

RIGHT: Stained glass abounds. It is in the main entrance door, the door to the bathroom, and under the ridge, on a hinged stained-glass panel leading to a storage loft.

neighbors and minimize noise along the section of common wall. Second, on the south end of the in-law was a small shed (2½ ft. by 9 ft.) that would be a great place to park a water heater.

So they decided to locate the kitchen and bathroom on the south end, sharing a *wet wall* (a wall containing water supply and drain pipes). It was a good choice. In addition to housing a water heater, the shed had enough room to create recessed bays for the refrigerator and a stacked washer-dryer in the bathroom. Both the bathroom and the kitchen (see the photos on pp. 192–193) are full size, which delighted the Sumners.

One other constraint led to a creative solution. The windows along the west wall look into the Sumners' courtyard, so its view is sunny and private. On the east, however, the in-law is hard against the property line. Windows on that side, even high up, would have encroached on their neighbor's privacy. And more windows would eat up precious wall space, which the Sumners

Beautiful wood warms the kitchen and eating areas: clear-grain fir windows, rift-cut white oak cabinets with ebony pulls, a solid teak table top, and teak banding to finish countertop edges. Under the bench seats there's room for storage.

ABOVE: Stacking the washer and dryer allowed the bathroom to double as a laundry room.

ONE WAY TO SOUNDPROOF THE SHARED WALL between a house and a bump-out unit is to install bookshelves after you've insulated the wall. A few hundred books have a lot of mass, which will discourage the transmission of sound.

desperately needed for closets and the Murphy bed. But without windows on the east, there would be no cross-ventilation. What to do?

The solution arrived in a blaze of light: operable skylights in the eastern side of the roof. When open, they allow cross-ventilation. Located over the Murphy bed, the skylights make the space feel like a big airy bedroom. And on clear nights, the Sumners can look at the stars and plan their next getaway. □

putting it all out there

Singer Jimmy Buffet once said that if you think of New Orleans as the northernmost city of the Caribbean it makes sense—the sultry climate, the gumbo of cultures, the live-and-let-live lifestyle. It's a place where the road less traveled needs an extra lane.

A CATHEDRAL TO NATURE

From time to time, the need to live large also inspires in-law suites, such as the one architect Dodie Smith designed on Pitt Street. From the street, the house looks like any other Greek Revival home built for a prosperous merchant or a

Viewed from the street, this 1870 New Orleans home is classic Greek Revival, with low pitched roofs, ornamental frieze and fascia trim, and slender columns on a wide porch that add a strong horizontal feeling.

Though the addition departs from some of the main house's architectural conventions, the two sections work together nicely.

The entrance to the in-law suite is dramatically vertical, with an oversized Palladian window tucked under its roof.

banker after the Civil War. Its low-pitched gable ends, slender columns, and wide porch are restful and predictable. Walk through the side gate, however, and things get a bit wild. Same colors, same clapboards, same trim as the old house. But the side porch looks as if it's about to launch off the steps, with a huge Palladian window going along for the flight (see the right photo above).

The addition was completed in 1988 and the clients moved on long ago, so Smith can't recall just why they wanted to add an in-law. But she does remember them as quiet, thoughtful people who loved nature, particularly an immense live oak in the side yard. So as Smith developed ideas for an addition that bumped out from the kitchen, her clients asked her to include the oak in the design.

The plan began as Smith envisioned a tiled passageway with windows on either side, running from the kitchen to a sunny sitting room at the back. A porch off the passageway opened into the side yard. From the sitting room, one could walk into a master bedroom and bath.

Given the 12-ft. ceilings of the old house and the demands of the climate, Smith had been thinking of a 15-ft. cathedral ceiling in the addition, so incorporating a 10-ft.-high Palladian window to frame the oak was not that much of a leap. And, this being New Orleans, if one dramatic opening was good, two would be even better. With a huge window in the porch entry and another in the bedroom wall, her clients would be able to lie in bed and look up, through two walls, into the oak's canopy (see the left photo on p. 197).

ADDING BATH AND KITCHEN VENT FANS to exhaust excess moisture from cooking or showering is essential to forestall mold, prevent rot, and protect the health of homeowners. But don't place exhaust ports under soffit vents because the moist air could be drawn into the attic.

Floor Plan

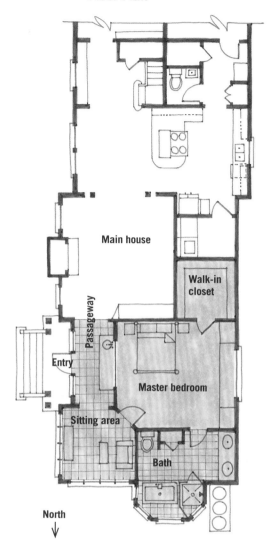

Main house

Walk-in closet

Passageway

Entry

Master bedroom

Sitting area

Bath

North
↓

A tiled passageway runs along the east side of the addition. A wet bar opposite the entrance allows gardeners in muddy shoes or grillers to pop in for a cold drink. At left, a second Palladian window looks into the master bedroom.

The owners loved it. So, following that ode to nature, they requested a master bathroom with so much clear glass it would be like showering outdoors (see the photo on the facing page).

A REFUGE FOR PARENTS

Realtors in other regions often advise homeowners not too get too outré when remodeling because flashy layouts might put off prospective buyers. In the Big Easy, however, outré is a badge of honor.

Some years later, when Larry Ponoroff, a law professor at Tulane and his wife, Monica, came upon the sprawling Pitt Street house and its expansive in-law suite, they imagined freedom of another kind. Their four kids, aged 7 to 12, could be safely housed in the four upstairs bedrooms toward the front of the old section. With that kind of spatial separation, Larry and Monica could enjoy peace and privacy they hadn't known in years. □

The master bedroom has 15-ft. cathedral ceilings and a clear view to a massive live oak in the side yard.

With windows on three walls, this bathroom has the feel of an outdoor shower, only more deluxe.

DEALING WITH HEAT AND HUMIDITY

Given New Orleans' tropical climate and its proximity to the Gulf, mitigating hot air and excess moisture is crucial to the comfort of its inhabitants and the health of its structures. Because the city is, on average, only a foot or two above sea level, its builders have long raised houses with tall foundations. The Pitt Street house is roughly 3½ ft. above grade, with latticed openings on all sides to ensure good crawlspace ventilation. A case can also be made for sealing and insulating a crawlspace and installing a dehumidifier to forestall rot, but the idea hasn't gained much traction in the Deep South, given the relative success of letting the air blow free.

Up above, gable-end vents, high ceilings, and fans are the methods most often used to deal with hot, humid air—with mixed success, because most of the heated air stays trapped inside. Historically, New Orleans builders have built roofs without roof overhangs and soffit vents, which means there's no place for fresh air to enter, rise as it heats, and exit at a high point in the roof. Consequently, many residents just shut the windows and crank up the AC. As one New Orleans native observed, "Folks will pay huge utility bills, but they won't address the issue of inadequate ventilation."

carving out options

T he Bridges were in the home stretch of designing a major renovation when they received an unsettling call from their daughter. Nothing definite yet, she told them, but if she and the baby needed to move in, could they? Of course, they told her. For as long as you need.

Shortly, they were meeting again with their architect to revisit layouts they had looked at dozens of times—though this time with new eyes. And there, in a cluster of three rooms on the west end of the house, they saw the solution to the problem that hadn't existed a week before. With only a few changes, they

Far from the street, a cluster of rooms over the garage was carved out as an in-law apartment. The exterior stairs were added to provide a separate entrance.

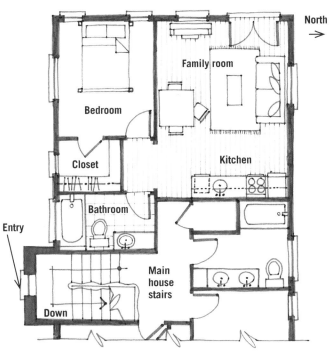

North →

Family room

Bedroom

Closet

Kitchen

Entry

Bathroom

Main house stairs

Down

View from the east. The three-bedroom house style is eclectic, with southern Mediterranean influences, most notably a limed stucco finish.

could carve out an in-law suite that would give their daughter as much privacy as she needed. Or as much company as she wanted.

THE SECRETS OF SHARED WALLS

Originally, the Bridges had envisioned the large room of the suite as a spacious family room because of its vaulted ceilings. Beyond that, there hadn't been much thought given to the family room's use—putting up guests, probably— but it became clear that with its own exterior entrance and a kitchen it could become a self-sufficient unit. There was an extra bedroom and a bath nearby, and an interior door that separated the cluster from the rest of the house.

The big question was where to put the kitchen. Fortunately, the wall opposite the new entrance was contiguous to a bathroom outside the proposed

FAUX WALLS

All the suite's walls were painted with a faux finish, in which several different hues are applied for greater depth of color. Though methods vary, a first color is often applied with a brush and a second accent color applied with an open-pore sponge. Faux painting imparts a patina of sorts and so is a very forgiving finish on walls whose surfaces are imperfect—frequently the case when a carve-out unit is created on a shoestring budget.

LEFT: At the other end of the great room is a modest kitchen. Because the wall behind is shared with a bathroom, it was easy to run wires, pipes, and ducts for kitchen appliances. At left, a boxed duct rises above the microwave and range.

BELOW: The bedroom on the southwest corner is sunny and serene. The architect specified narrow-muntin metal windows set in the 2x6 walls to expose more of the sill and emphasize the wall's thickness.

FACING PAGE: The vaulted ceiling makes the room feel spacious and the dormers give it drama.

suite. That shared wall, already plumbed for a bathroom, was the logical place to run the plumbing, wiring, and exhaust ducts a kitchen needed. Moreover, soundproofing the shared wall wouldn't take much. Plans already called for cast-iron DWV pipes, which suppress sounds, and an insulated 2x6 wall would dampen them still further. Nor was noise an issue for the suite's bathroom, for it backed up against a set of stairs.

Because their daughter's plans remained in flux, it made little sense to chop up the space and create an enclosed kitchen—it would have been dark—so the Bridges settled on a bank of cabinets with various appliances tucked into them. Drawing on southern Mediterranean influences found throughout the house, they chose wood-grained cabinets with a glazed finish and precast concrete countertops, which are easy to maintain. The backsplash tiles are concrete as well.

Though they had carved out the apartment with their daughter in mind, the Bridges took permits and got the suite approved as a legal in-law unit, as if to say, "Hope for the best, but be ready for whatever comes." □

peaceful coexistence

A ccording to neighborhood lore, the attic of this 1908 single-story house was converted to living space some time in the 1930s when, instead of divorcing, the couple that owned it separated and the husband moved upstairs. It must have been like moving from the frying pan into the broiler, given the absence of any insulation in the attic. And so the attic remained—freezing cold in winter, roasting hot in summer—until the mid-1990s, when its present owner transformed it into the comfortable rental it is today. If you've been thinking about converting an unfinished attic, you'll appreciate the inventive solutions that Alan Jencks, a master carpenter, brought to this renovation.

ABOVE: A handsome oriel window on the main house overlooks the path to the in-law entrance. For privacy within and without, the oriel's glass is frosted.

By barely changing the roof profile, the owners of this attic in-law kept the goodwill of their neighbors. Set well back from the street, the roof deck is hardly noticeable.

Little changed by the renovation, the living room still has its original built-ins.

These stair-side bookcases were originally planned so they would face into the living room—where they would have been blocked by a couch. Turning bookcases toward the stair is a perfect way to remind yourself of that book you've been meaning to read.

A WORKABLE PLAN

Jencks began with a general plan and worked things out as he went. He had three objectives: maximize the size of the living space, minimize changes to the roof profile so neighbors wouldn't be rattled, and make it nice. An apartment with thoughtful finish details would attract better tenants, command a higher rent, and accommodate the owners' dreams of moving into the attic themselves someday, renting out the downstairs, and traveling.

Because the banished husband had been living only in the back half of the attic, there was a lot of room for expansion. (The front half of the attic was unfinished storage space so jammed with stuff that the ceiling below bellied 3 in.) Revising the layout was straightforward. The living room kept its

Floor Plan

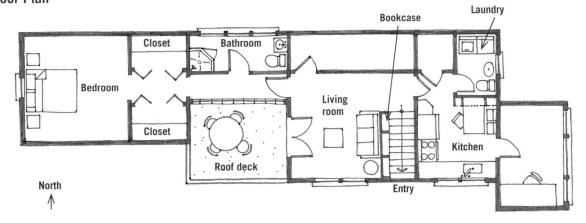

North ↑

CAST-IRON PIPE IS FAR BETTER THAN PLASTIC PIPE for suppressing the sound of rushing water. When waste pipes run near public areas such as dining rooms, using cast-iron pipes can spare you and your guests the sound of a toilet flushing.

ABOVE: Except for a curved valance added to soften the area around the sink, the kitchen is largely unchanged since the 1930s. The home office at left was once a sleeping porch.

FACING PAGE: These fold-down seats and table were prefab elements widely available in the '30s and '40s for compact kitchens in in-law apartments.

WATCH YOUR HEADROOM

In the unfinished part of the attic, 2x6 floor joists spanned almost 18 ft. Adding a bearing wall underneath would have shortened the span but that solution would have bisected the master bedroom downstairs. Another approach, nailing a 2x12 to the side of each 2x6—known as *sistering*—wouldn't have worked either because it would have reduced headroom in the attic. In the end, Jencks bolstered each 2x6 joist by bolting a predrilled, ¼-in.-thick by 5-in.-wide steel *flitch plate* to the side of it. Because steel has a greater load-bearing capacity than wood, steel members don't need to be as deep as wood joists.

existing location. The kitchen stayed put (and was left mostly untouched) to minimize expensive pipe re-routing. The old bathroom became a laundry, and the storage space was converted to a bedroom, a hallway flanked by closets, a full bathroom with shower, and a roof deck (see the top photo on p. 207). The tricky part of the remodel was re-framing the attic. The rafters and floor joists were 2x6s—seriously undersized for the distances they spanned and the loads they carried.

Because the remodel was extensive, Jencks divided the work into two phases. During the first phase, he gutted the interior, bolstered the structure, framed new walls, upgraded wiring and plumbing, insulated between rafters, and took steps to dampen sound transmission through the floor. In the second phase, he stripped the roof, added rigid insulation outside, and installed new roofing. Normally re-roofing is not such a big deal, but this roof hadn't been stripped in 90 years and the weight of several tons of old roofing compromised the strength of the structure.

WASTE NOT, WANT NOT

When renovating, you can save time and money by using existing materials whenever possible—especially plumbing systems, whose large waste pipes are often difficult to re-route. After the fixtures in the old bathroom were removed, the cast-iron pipes that remained were suitable drains for the new clothes washer. In the new bathroom, Jencks was able to route drainpipes

between joists, down through a closet on the first floor, and then into the crawlspace, where they connected to the main drain. He was also conservative when framing the new bathroom: A simple shed dormer instead of a more complicated gable dormer provided adequate headroom without substantially altering the roof profile.

QUIET FLOORS AND STAIRS

Unfinished attics are usually easy to insulate unless the floorboards are nailed down. Remove any stored items, install acoustic insulation, then install the finish floor system. Alternately, you can pull up floorboards or drill a hole at the end of each joist bay and blow in cellulose insulation. If there is any blocking between joists, you'll have uninsulated spots but, overall, it's a reasonable solution.

If there are interior stairs, do your best to soundproof them, too. Because the stairs at this project were excessively steep and flimsy, Jencks tore them

WHEN SOUNDPROOFING, don't forget that vibrating appliances can make a lot of racket. Under the refrigerator in the attic, Jencks installed the type of thin foam pad typically used under floating floors, covering that with ¼-in. plywood underlayment and, finally, resilient flooring. The washer and dryer are mounted on a platform fastened to the steel-spring-and-neoprene vibration isolators often used to mount commercial cooling units to roofs.

The sloping ceilings on either side of the hallway are a perfect height for clothes storage. The louvers allow air to circulate so clothes won't get musty. The curved peak of the ceiling makes the bedroom feel hand-crafted and cozy.

out and constructed new ones. To dampen the sound of footfalls, he first used standard fiberglass batts to insulate the underside. (Some types of fiberglass batts are sold as sound-attenuating insulation.) That done, he covered the underside of the stair carriage with two layers of drywall. He used ½-in.- and ⅝-in.-thick sheets because different thicknesses vibrate at different frequencies (for more on sound mitigation, see p. 47).

TAKE THE AIR

Jencks had two opportunities to insulate the roof. When he gutted the interior, he added fiberglass batts between rafters. Later, when he stripped old roofing down to the sheathing, he bolted new 2x4s on-edge to the top of sagging 2x4 rafters to stiffen them. Then he installed 3½-in. rigid insulation panels between the new 2x4s. Finally, he nailed roof sheathing into place and installed new shingles. Thanks to those two layers of insulation, the attic is now pleasant year-round.

Jencks improved ventilation by installing exhaust fans in both the kitchen and the bathroom. To allow excessively hot air under the roof to escape, he installed ridge vents. To increase cross-ventilation in the master bedroom, he added a double-hung window in the gable end wall and an openable skylight in the far corner of the room. And the roof deck is a great place to catch a breeze on a warm day. □

A modest shed dormer provided enough room for this comfortable bathroom. Not wanting to install a vanity, the owners opted for a tiled shelf instead.

a safe place to land

Originally built as a single-family dwelling in 1906, the house was a duplex when Lucy and Ned Holmes found it in the 1970s. A previous owner had added a door at the top of the front stairs to separate the units and installed a little strip of a kitchen in the hallway upstairs. The setup lacked finesse, but income from the upstairs apartment enabled the Holmes to buy the house. Ned was in law school at the time and money was tight.

Sunday brunch at home. After several different incarnations, the attic in-law unit is now, happily, a landing pad for an adult daughter. The unit's exterior stairs, just visible at right, give it second means of egress and access to the backyard. The garage, at left, houses a shared laundry.

UNDOING A DUPLEX

When Lucy and Ned began raising a family, they removed the makeshift entrance, converted the upstairs kitchen into closets and built-in cabinets, and put a washer-dryer on the second floor. Other than that, the conversion back to a single-family house was straightforward. With two active daughters, though, they were cramped for space so they added a large room off the back of the first floor, which became a family room and, later, a master bedroom. And for good measure, they built a deck above it. With an eye to future uses, they also added exterior stairs off the deck so that the upstairs would have a second egress if it ever became an in-law again.

REDOING AN IN-LAW

By the time the girls had grown up and moved into places of their own, the house was showing its age and it became clear that if they didn't renovate it extensively, Ned would be repairing it piecemeal till the end of time. They no longer needed storage for four people, so Lucy and Ned decided that it was time to convert the second floor back into an in-law, though this time, an in-law nice enough for their daughters or themselves to live in someday. The in-law would be a safe place for the daughters to land whenever they were "in between things."

Once again, the original floor plan remained more or less intact, with a large bedroom at either end of the second floor. After the space was gutted and new drywall was up, they turned their attention to the new kitchen. To gain space, the Holmes moved the washer and dryer into the garage. They

After bumping out an addition to create a master bedroom on the first floor, the homeowners topped it with a second-story deck for the in-law. The decking and railings are made of clear-heart redwood, finished with spar varnish, and nicely detailed—note the shaped railings—for a somewhat dressier look. Railings and balusters are essential to second-story safety, so they might as well look good.

ROOF DECK DETAILS

Roof decks are a great asset, in part because of the views they afford. Because they are typically situated over living spaces, however, you must take special care to avoid leaks. Here are a few important details:

Size roof decks for live loads. Have an engineer size the ceiling joists supporting the deck for live loads—the people who will be standing on and moving across the deck. Joists that are too small could damage finish surfaces below and compromise the roof membrane.

Play it safe. Local building codes specify deck railing heights—typically, 42 in. high—and other safety details. Heed them: Nobody ever plans to fall off a roof deck.

Provide for drainage. Even a so-called flat roof has a slight pitch so water can run off it. And water has to be directed away from building façades and foundations via drains or gutters and downspouts.

Protect the roof membrane. An elastomeric waterproof membrane protects the roof under the deck and prevents water damage below. Great care must be taken to keep decking and the people on it from damaging that membrane.

IF YOU LIVE IN A TEMPERATE CLIMATE and your garage is enclosed, consider putting your washer and dryer there. If it's a shared laundry, it will be accessible to all occupants, won't eat up precious living space inside, and the machines' noise won't disturb anyone.

removed a window that had long bothered them because it looked right into a neighbor's house, and replaced it with a skylight. Finally, they installed new cabinets, counters, and appliances—a full-size stove and refrigerator because Ned and their youngest daughter are serious cooks. The only concession to the tight space is a half-width dishwasher.

By the time the unit was complete, their older daughter returned from working in Germany with a new beau in tow. And after she moved to her own place, her sister moved in. Family life is, as always, a work in progress. Now when Ned and Lucy settle in for the night, their youngest is often getting ready to go out with friends. Her bedroom is on the other end of the house, however, so she rarely disturbs her parents. And when Ned and Lucy get up early on weekends, as is their custom, they aren't likely to wake their daughter.

Floor Plan

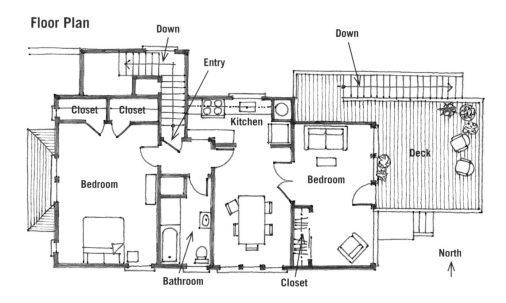

Kitchen clutter is largely concealed by walls separating it from the living area. At right is the entrance to the bedroom. When louvered door shades are open, natural light from the bedroom floods what would otherwise be a dark portion of the living area; when closed they ensure privacy.

Attic in-laws can have wonderful angles and light. Here, a window over the sink, which looked directly into a neighbor's second floor, was replaced with a skylight. It provides more light, more room for shelves, and much more privacy.

BEING A LANDLORD IS A TRICKY BALANCE of keeping an eye on things without intruding. So if something breaks, tenants should report it promptly and landlords, fix it cheerfully. When your landlord is your father, communication is even more crucial.

appendix: universal design

Universal design attempts to create public spaces, private residences, products—whatever—that are accessible to and usable by the greatest number of people, regardless of their age or physical condition. Although the concept is often associated with the needs of disabled people, a superior design is easier to use by everyone. A wider doorway, for example, is as welcome to a mother with a baby on her hip as it is to someone in a walker. Here are some universal design guidelines for your in-law.

LIVING AREAS

Exterior doors should be 36 in. wide and all interior doors should have at least 32 in. of clearance between the jambs when open. Both sides of an entrance need a clear area at least 5 ft. by 5 ft. so a person in a wheelchair can maneuver. Keep thresholds low (¼ in., maximum) or eliminate them altogether if you can. Generous overhangs over exterior doors will help keep water out. Speaking of doors, eliminate interior doors whenever they aren't essential. Hinged doors are particularly problematic because their swings create *dead areas*— nearly 16½ sq. ft. of floor space per door that can't be used for anything else. Besides, opening and closing hinged doors is taxing for someone on wheels. *Pocket doors* or *gliding doors* on barn-door hardware are easier to operate and take up almost no floor space.

Window dimensions are as important, especially where they serve as emergency egress.

Building codes often specify that egress windows be at least 24 in. high and 20 in. wide, with a net-clear opening (an opening unobstructed by sash, muntins, or window frame) of at least 5.7 sq. ft. But people who can't bend their legs need wider egress—say, windows 30 in. wide. Similarly, though codes allow a maximum sill height of 44 in. for egress windows, a sill height of 18 in. to 20 in. is preferable for someone in a wheelchair (wheelchair seats are 18 in. to 20 in. high).

BATHROOMS

A typical in-law is already a small space, and providing accessible bathroom spaces can be a challenge. One of the most space-efficient and safe bathroom designs is a wet room, in which the showering area is not enclosed by a wall or a curb (see photos on p. 106 and p. 174). Several elements are necessary for a fully functional special-needs bathroom:

- **A wide door,** preferably 36 in., with no threshold. A door on a sliding track is easier to open and close than a hinged door, and takes up less space.
- **Enough room inside** to maneuver a wheelchair, which means a 5-ft.-wide circle of clear space in which a wheelchair can maneuver. There must be enough room to approach and use each fixture. If there is open space under a sink counter, this space can be included in the radius. Basically, the 5-ft. turning circle is the universal standard for a

wheelchair-accessible bathroom: a disabled person can pull into the middle of, say, a bathroom with fixtures on three walls and have enough room to turn the wheelchair 360 degrees and approach each fixture. There must be enough space alongside the toilet to enable transfers back and forth.

- **Grab bars** screwed or bolted to wall framing or to ¾-in. plywood under finished surfaces. Small bathrooms with grab bars are very safe for people unsteady on their feet because there is always a grab bar within arm's length to hold on to.
- **Countertop height** of no more than 32 in. and deep enough (20 in.) to admit a wheelchair user's legs beneath; that height allows a seated person to use the sink easily.
- **Textured floor surfaces** throughout the area. Bathroom floors must be hard and impervious so they can be easily cleaned, but they shouldn't be slick when wet. A little bit of texture decreases the chance of a fall.
- **Shower seats** should be 18 in. high and be made of a non-slip material. If the person in your in-law unit prefers a tub to a shower, investigate walk-in tubs.

KITCHENS

When designing a kitchen for a person with limited mobility, keep in mind the optimal reach zone of someone seated in a wheelchair: 20 in. to 44 in. above the ground. Less-used objects can be stored outside this range but the kitchen will be safest and best-utilized if commonly used cooking supplies and appliances can be located in this zone. Happily, many manufacturers offer undercounter appliances such as drawer refrigerators, and other appliances small enough to fit on a lower shelf or countertop. To improve access, many designers specify cabinet drawers instead of fixed lower shelves obscured by doors. A well-designed kitchen should have:

- **Wide aisles** to work in and move through. Ideally, there should be at least 42-in. to 48-in. clearance in front of work counters and appliances. In the center of the kitchen there should be a 60-in. turning circle in which a wheelchair can maneuver. If there will be two cooks in the kitchen, work aisles should be 48 in. to 60 in. wide.
- **Countertops 32 in.** high, which are right in the middle of that optimal reach zone. This makes them the ideal height for a seated cook. Include as much counterspace as possible. Especially important are set-down areas on either side of a sink, a cooktop, and an oven. These are places where cooks can temporarily park a heavy pot and should be at least 30 in. wide.

- **Neutral handedness.** Whether cooks are right- or left-handed, they should be able to approach and operate an appliance from their strongest side. Many appliances can be installed with right- or left-mounted door hinges.
- **Enough knee room.** Under-counter areas should be at least 20 in. deep so someone in a wheelchair can pull in close to the counter.
- **Pull-out storage.** The beauty of pull-out drawers in lower cabinets is that items once stranded in the back of the cabinet can now be reached easily. Vertical, pull-out pantries hold a ton of stuff; reserve upper shelves for foods with a long shelf life.
- **Lower your uppers.** By lowering upper cabinets so that their lowest shelves are 12 in. to 15. in. above the countertop, you'll make items stored on them easier to reach by short people or folks with limited range. (Range hoods should stay 24 in. to 30 in. above stoves or cooktops, however.)

- **Accessible appliances.** Keep appliances within the optimal reach zone of 20 in. to 44 in. above the floor. The cooktop should be mounted on a 32-in.-high counter. A single row of burners is best so a seated cook won't have to reach over a hot front burner to reach one in the back. Ideally, the cooktop's control will be on a front panel. A wall oven with side-swing door (similar to a microwave door) is much easier to access than a standard drop-down oven door. Mount the wall oven so its base is 32 in. above the floor, and make sure it has a self-cleaning feature. A microwave is small, so it can sit on a countertop or be built-in under the counter. The dishwasher should be front-loading, with its controls on the front of the machine. Compact dishwashers or models with half-load wash options are best for single tenants. Refrigerator drawers and freezer drawers fit nicely under a counter and are more efficient than front-opening models because cool air doesn't fall out of the freezer when the door is opened.

UNIVERSAL CONTROLS

A big step toward improving accessibility is installing electrical and plumbing controls that everyone can operate, including people with limited strength or chronic conditions such as arthritis, which makes grasping and turning objects difficult and often painful.

Rocker switches, push-buttons, and toggle switches are electrical controls that are easy to use, whereas a standard dial-rheostat or a lamp with a twist-knob switch could be a problem for some. Door hardware such as D-pulls and lever handles is favored by people with impaired strength; twist doorknobs and thumb-latches are agony because they require a tight grip to operate the mechanism. Hot and cold tap handles that must be twisted are harder to operate than lever handles. Larger paddle levers can be operated with an elbow or forearm, which is also handy if your hands are dirty. Some faucets even have touch-sensitive spouts or handles, such as those with Delta's Touch20® technology; it turns on if you touch it anywhere on the spout or handle. Infra-red control sensors once seen only in airport bathrooms now grace residential bathrooms.

resources

MORE INFORMATION ABOUT ADUS

The Internet is awash with articles about finding, vetting, and hiring architects and contractors; no need to spend much time on that here. Self-help titles and contract forms from legal publishers such as www.nolopress.com are great resources, as are articles from popular trade publications such as Fine Homebuilding *and* The Journal of Light Construction. *Among specialty online bookstores, www.buildersbooksource.com is about the best, offering titles on every aspect of designing and building, including codes, and contracts. Many state agencies also offer free online resources. The California State License Board, for one, has great information about issues to address in a contract.*

SMART GROWTH AND ADU SITES

By searching "smart growth" or "accessory dwelling units" you can find extensive resources online; many are free. Here's a sample:

AARP Public Policy Institute has long advocated revised zoning codes that encourage the building of in-law units, especially for seniors. www.aarp.org/research/ppi/

The City of Santa Cruz ADU Development Program offers a free ADU manual and sells prototype ADU plans: www.cityofsantacruz.com/index. aspx?page=1150

ARCH. A regional coalition for housing based in King County, WA. Their site offers a great walk-through of the ADU process: www.archhousing.org/adu2/

Smart Growth Online. A national clearinghouse of smart growth initiatives and resources. http://smartgrowth.org/about/default.asp

U.S. Department of Housing and Urban Development (HUD). Offers an overview of in-law units in the U.S., with appendices that show zoning regulations in different regions. www.huduser.org/Publications/PDF/adu.pdf

Canada Mortgage and Housing Corporation's huge site offers "innovative solutions to housing challenges," including green, universal design, ADUs, etc. cmhc-schl.gc.ca/

SMALL-HOUSE AND ADU PLANS

The sites listed below include information clearinghouses and for-profit companies that sell small-house plans and/or prebuilt cottages.

The Tiny House Blog is a good place to start if you're thinking of an in-law cottage for your property. It includes links to tiny houses, log cabins, and green shelter. http://tinyhouseblog.com/

Tiny House Design is focused on extreme downsizing solutions for people looking to move to a more sustainable and simple lifestyle. www.tinyhousedesign.com

Tumbleweed Tiny House Company offers house plans and houses from 65 sq. ft. to 837 sq. ft. www.tumbleweedhouses.com/

Little House on a Trailer offers plans and handsomely detailed little houses which they will customize to match a house on your property. http://thelittlehouseonthetrailer.com/

New Avenue Homes offers property owners a turn-key solution by taking care of financing, permitting, and construction of ADUs nationwide. A wave of the future? www.newavenuehomes.com/

GREEN RESOURCES

There are many sources of information, but two general sites are good places to start. One (www.greenbuildingadvisor. com) bills itself as a complete source for building, designing, and remodeling green houses. GBA accepts no advertising, so its product reviews are as objective as its categories are broad. The EPA/DOE's www.energystar.org is another omnibus website, with links to home energy audit information and green tax credit guides; there's also a search engine that allows you to compare the efficiency ratings of various appliance models.

SPECIAL-NEEDS RESOURCES

The clearinghouse site http://www.ada. gov/ has a wealth of resources. You can, for example, download a copy of "ADA Standards for Accessible Design," which has specifications for ADA-compliant bath and kitchen layouts. You may also find useful Building for a Lifetime: The Design and Construction of Fully Accessible Homes *(Taunton Press e-book, 2009).*

OTHER ADU RESOURCES

Any website that offers good information about building products and construction techniques will be helpful as you design and plan your in-law. However, the following resources are especially useful for ADUs.

Basement insulation. Companies such as Basement Systems (www. basementsystems.com) and Owens Corning (www.owenscorningbasements. com) offer modular finishing systems that combine insulation, water-resistant panels, and the like. They must be installed by licensed professionals. Homeowners determined to do their own basement conversions might want to look into the InSoFast system (www.insofast.com).

Disappearing beds. This is just a sampling of resources; many others are available.

Complete plans, materials, hardware, and lifting mechanisms to build a bed that converts into a drop-leaf desk during daylight hours. www.rockler.com

The Murphy Bed™ Company (still run by a Murphy) offers a wide range of models "raised and lowered effortlessly by a spring-loaded counter-balancing system." www.murphybedcompany.com

In-law owners with low ceilings and "green" sensibilities may want to look into the Mission Horizontal Murphy bed constructed entirely from FSC-certified woods. www.wallbedfactory.com

Vertical- and horizontal-opening beds set in custom cabinetry can be ordered from Flying Beds; it also acts as a distributor for European makers such as SmartBeds of Italy and LiftBed®, the German company whose beds hide in ceilings. The website also discusses the merits of different lifting mechanisms (gas piston, compression coils, sequential cold steel springs, electric motor-driven beds) and offers a list of questions that will be helpful to comparison shoppers. www. flyingbeds.com

PRODUCT MANUFACTURERS

The manufacturers below have been chosen because they offer kitchen and bath products that make the most of small spaces, can be used by people with disabilities or limited strength, or are exceptionally water- and energy-conscious.

APPLIANCES

These manufacturers offer energy-efficient or compact kitchen and laundry appliances.
www.amana.com
www.boschappliances.com
www.elmirastoveworks.com
www.fisherpaykel.com
www.geappliances.com
www.jennair.com
www.kenmore.com
www.kitchenaid.com
www.lge.com
www.liebherr.us
www.maytag.com
www.subzero.com
www.thermador.com
www.whirlpool.com

TOILETS

These companies make small-size, speciality toilets (such as macerating toilets) or highly efficient water-conserving toilets. And some make a slightly higher toilet so wheelchair users can easily transfer to the toilet and back.
www.americanstandard.com
www.bemismfg.com
www.bigjohntoiletseat.com
www.briggsplumbing.com
www.brondell.com
www.caromausa.com
www.duravit.com
www.eljer.com
www.gerberonline.com
www.totousa.com
www.greatjohns.com
www.saniflo.com

SHOWER AND SINK HARDWARE

These suppliers offer offset (space-conserving) and easy-use lever faucets.
www.alsons.com
www.americanstandard.com
www.brilliantshowers.com
www.danze.com
www.dornbracht.com
www.grohe.com
www.hansgrohe.com
www.kohler.com
www.moen.com
www.oxygenics.com

www.pfister.com
www.pricepulseshowerspas.com
www.rohlhome.com

KITCHEN FAUCETS

These companies offer lever-handle kitchen faucets, and some offer no-hands controls.
www.americanstandard.com
www.aquadis.com
www.blancoamerica.com
www.chicagofaucets.com
www.danze-online.com
www.deltafaucet.com
www.dornbracht.com
www.elkayusa.com
www.groheamerica.com
www.hamatusa.com

MICROWAVES

Microwaves are great space-savers and are very well suited to use in an in-law.
www.amana.com
www.kitchenaid.com
www.lgappliances.com
www.maytag.com
www.panasonic.com
www.samsung.com
www.sharpusa.com
www.whirlpool.com

SMALL BATH RESOURCES

Here you'll find manufacturers of very small sinks, corner sinks, and other space-saving products.
www.americanstandard.com
www.batesandbates.com
www.dornbracht.com
www.duravit.com
www.elizabethanclassics.com
www.eljer.com
www.faucet.com
www.hansgrohe.com
www.kallista.com
www.kohler.com
www.neo-metro.com
www.porcher-us.com
www.robern.com
www.rockymountainhardware.com
www.stoneforest.com
www.totousa.com

DISHWASHERS

All of these companies make half-size, slender, and drawer-type dishwashers for tight-space applications.
www.askousa.com
www.bosch-home.com
www.fisherpaykel.com
www.gaggenau.com
www.geappliances.com
www.kitchenaid.com

www.maytag.com
www.miele.com
www.whirlpool.com

SPACE-OPTIMIZING KITCHEN STORAGE

To make the most out of what limited storage is available in an in-law, check these sources for a variety of kitchen and bath storage solutions.
www.ccfdrawers.com
www.hafele.com/us
www.kitchensource.com
www.kv.com
www.rev-a-shelf.com
www.shelvesthatslide.com
www.householdessential.com

COMPACT KITCHEN RESOURCES

If you need the most kitchen in the smallest space, here's where to find it.
www.acmekitchenettes.com
www.ajmadison.com
www.avantiproducts.com
www.cleverkitchen.de
www.compact-kitchens.com
www.compactappliances.com
www.dwyerkitchens.com
www.ikea.com
www.yestertec.com

KEEP IN TOUCH!

While researching *In-laws, Outlaws, and Granny Flats*, I found a ton of great stuff that we had no room for in the book. And I'm finding more every day. So please join my online family. Visit my blog and website to see great outtakes and daily updates.

All the best,
Mike Litchfield
www.cozydigz.blogspot.com
www.cozydigz.com

designers, architects, and contractors

pp. 4, 5 Architect: Lynn Hopkins, www.lhopkinsarch.com, **Contractor:** Loren French, Summit Builders

pp. 6, 35 Architect: Sim Van der Ryn, www.vanderryn.com

pp. 7, 9 Designer: Stephen Shoup, www.buildinglab.com, **Contractor:** Building Lab

pp. 14–19 Renovation design: Architectural Resources Group, www.argsf.com

pp. 21, 81 Architect: Lynn Hopkins, www.lhopkinsarch.com, **Contractor:** Loren French, Summit Builders

p. 22 Landscape Design: Lisa and Tim Goodman, www.goodmanlandscape.com

pp. 25, 84 Architect: Steve Rynerson, www.rynersonobrien.com, **Contractor:** Dana Milner

p. 28 Architect: D. Michael Danielson, Evergreen Architecture, **Contractor:** R.C. Humphrey Construction

pp. 30, 125–128 Architect: Ron Brenner, www.larsonbrenner.com, **Contractor:** Herman Renovation Company

p. 41 Architect: Michael Fifield, Fifield Architecture + Urban Design

pp. 43, 90–95 Architect: John McKelvey, www.andmck.com, **Contractor:** Boa Constructor Building & Design

pp. 44–49 Architect: Jon Larson, www.jarvisarchitects.com, **Contractor:** Camber Construction

pp. 50,188–193 Designer/builder: Beth and Gary Sumner

p. 59 (bottom) Architect: Cheryl Mohr, Amy Gardner, www.gardnermohr.com

pp. 60, 63 Designer: Marcy Voyevod, www.marcyvoyevod.com, **Contractor:** Blue Lotus

pp. 68–73 Architects: Frederick Hyer, Patricia Fontana-Narell, www.hyerarchitecture.com, **Contractor:** Canivet Construction

p. 74 Designer/builder: Jeff Hellerman, www.goodwincreekfarm.com, **Contractor:** Tim Feazell

p. 78 Restoration: John Michael Davis

p. 80 Designer/builder: Stephen Marshall, www.thelittlehouseonthetrailer.com

p. 83 Architect: George Ostrow, Velocipede Architects, www.velocipede.net, **Contractor:** Stonewood Builders/Borromeo Construction

p. 86 Architects: Roxana Vargas Greenan, Trent Greenan, www.vargasgreenan.com, **Contractor:** Prairie View Homes

pp. 89, 162–165 Architect: Russell Hamlet, AIA, www.studiohamlet.com, **Contractor:** Geoffrey Hobert Builders

pp. 97–101 Designer/builder: Dean Rutherford, www.ruthandsing.com

pp. 108–111 Architect: Fran Halperin, www.halperinandchrist.com, **Contractor:** Eric Christ

pp. 112–117 Architect: James Tuer, AIA, www.jwtarchitecture.com, **Contractor:** Wood Bros. Construction

pp. 119–124 Architect: Arleta Chang, www.jarvisarchitects.com, **Contractor:** Zanderbuilt

pp. 129–133 Architect: Robin Pennell, www.jarvisarchitects.com, **Contractor:** Whitney Collins Builder

pp. 134–139 Architect: Michael Klement, AIA, www.architecturalresource.com, **Contractor:** Donald Huff, Home Renewal Inc.

pp. 141–144 Designer/builders: Tolya and Otto Stonorov, www.stonorovworkshop.com

pp. 145–149 Architect: Anne Phillips, AIA, www.aparch.com, **Contractor:** Winans Construction

pp. 150–155 Architect: Joanne Koch, AIA, www.kocharchitects.com

pp. 156–161 Architect: Russell Hamlet, AIA, www.studiohamlet.com, **Contractor:** Even Construction

pp. 170–174 Architect: Jerri Holan, FAIA, www.holanarchitects.com, **Contractor:** Kiefer Construction

pp. 175–181 Architect: John Hopkins, AIA, www.hopkinstudio.com, **Contractor:** Cerami Builders

pp. 183–187 Architect: Steve Rynerson, www.rynersonobrien.com, **Contractor:** Jetton Construction

pp. 194–197 Architect: C. Spencer Smith, AIA, www.charlottespencersmith.com, **Contractor:** John Michael Davis

pp. 198–201 Architect: Fran Halperin, www.halperinandchrist.com, **Contractor:** Eric Christ

pp. 202–207, 208–211 Designer/builder: Alan Jencks, www.alanjencks.com

photo credits

All photos by Muffy Kibbey, except as noted below:

pp. 2, 6, 25, 35, 57, 77, 88, 142: by Michael Litchfield

pp. 4–5, 83: Charles Bickford, courtesy *Fine Homebuilding*, © The Taunton Press, Inc.

pp. 15, 19 (bottom): courtesy Point Reyes National Park Service

pp. 21, 81: Eric Roth

p. 22: Lisa Goodman

p. 28: Karen Timm

p. 30, 127–128: Greg Auseth

p. 41: mikedeanphoto.com

p. 45: Jon Larson

p. 50: David Simone

p. 51: Fisher & Paykel

pp. 52, 175–179, 181: Chuck Miller, courtesy *Fine Homebuilding*, © The Taunton Press, Inc.

p. 54: YesterTec Design

p. 55: (top and bottom left) Häfele; **(bottom right)** Rev-a-Shelf

p. 59: (top) Safety Tubs; **(bottom)** Cheryl Mohr

p. 60: (left) GROHE

p. 61: TOTO

p. 67: Rockler.com

p. 75: Jeff Hellerman

p. 75: Ken Gutmaker

p. 78: Theresa Cassagne

p. 79: Kathryn DeLaszlo

p. 84: (before photo) Steve Rynerson; **(after photo)** Ken Gutmaker

p. 86: John Ross, courtesy *Fine Homebuilding*, © The Taunton Press, Inc.

p. 89: Art Grice

pp. 91–92: David Foster

p. 97: (top) Dean Rutherford

pp. 112–117: Art Grice

p. 126: courtesy Heidi Bye

p. 129: (top) Robin Pennell

pp. 134–137: Beth Singer

p. 138: (top) Cheryl Hall; **(bottom)** Beth Singer

pp. 141, 143–144: Aya Brackett

pp. 156–165: Art Grice

p. 170: (top) Jerri Holan

p. 183: (top) Art Hartinger

pp. 188, 191–193: David Simone

pp. 189–190: Beth Sumner

pp. 194–197: Theresa Cassagne

index